Selected Poems

EDMUND BLUNDEN (1896–1974) grew up in Kent and went to school in Sussex at Christ's Hospital; these were the formative landscapes of his boyhood. He joined the Royal Sussex Regiment in 1915, serving in France and Flanders. His collection *The Shepherd* (1922) made his reputation as a poet; his classic account of his military service, *Undertones of War* (1928) was written while he was teaching in Japan. He made his living by writing and editing, with two extended periods of teaching: as a Fellow of Merton College 1931–42, and as Professor of English at the University of Hong Kong 1953–64. He received the Queen's Gold Medal for Poetry in 1956, and was Professor of Poetry at the University of Oxford 1966–68. His passions were poetry, book collecting, cricket, and the English countryside; he was haunted by his war experience all his life.

ROBYN MARSACK began her long association with Carcanet Press by editing the first edition of Edmund Blunden's *Selected Poems* in 1982, and worked as a publishers' editor until she became Director of the Scottish Poetry Library 2000–2016. She was a Royal Literary Fund Writing Fellow at the University of Glasgow 2016–2018. She has co-edited several poetry anthologies, including *OxfordPoets 2013* with Iain Galbraith, and edited Blunden's *Fall In, Ghosts: selected war prose*, published by Carcanet in 2014.

T0294120

Also by EDMUND BLUNDEN
from Carcanet Press

Fall In, Ghosts: selected war prose
edited by Robyn Marsack

EDMUND BLUNDEN

Selected Poems

edited by Robyn Marsack

Carcanet
Classics

First published in Great Britain in 2018 by
Carcanet Press Ltd
Alliance House, 30 Cross Street
Manchester M2 7AQ
www.carcanet.co.uk

A CIP catalogue record for this book is available
from the British Library: ISBN 978 1 784 10687 4

The publisher acknowledges financial assistance
from Arts Council England

Typeset in England by XL Publishing Services, Exmouth
Printed and bound in England by SRP Ltd, Exeter

Contents

To Nature (1923)

Masks of Time (1925)

English Poems (1926)

Poems 1930–1940 (1941)

Shells By a Stream (1944)

After the Bombing and other short poems (1949)

Poems of Many Years (1957)

A Hong Kong House: poems 1951–1961 (1962)

Eleven Poems (1965)

Introduction

… my experiences in the First World War have haunted me
all my life and for many days I have, it seems,
lived in that world rather than this.[1]

As the official commemoration of the First World War comes to a close in the centennial year of 2018, this selection of Edmund Blunden's poems raises a question: can we draw a line, even a hundred years after the event, and say, 'It's over'? For this soldier-poet it was never over, and his poems show us that, long after the battles were lost and won, memories of war could crowd out everything else. This is how war works, leaving its indelible traces on the mind as well as the body. Remembrance is traumatic, involuntary, and yet curiously welcome: 'I know that I did better one or two nights on the River Ancre than I ever can with my ink bottle', Blunden wrote to his friend Siegfried Sassoon.[2] His pen, though, has helped to shape subsequent generations' perception of the Great War.

Edmund Blunden grew up with a love of rivers – 'Happily through my years this small stream ran; / It charmed the boy…' ('Epitaph') – and the beginning of his life could scarcely have been more idyllic. Although he was born in London, in 1896, and had an enduring affection for the city, in 1900 his father became headmaster of a Church of England primary school in Yalding, Kent: here the ground of Blunden's imagination was established. Here was village England in its heyday: the twelfth-century church, where Charles Blunden was choirmaster and played the organ; the village street, a mix of cottages and eighteenth-century houses; the River Medway and its tributaries for angling; hopfields and orchards; a watermill at Cheveney; cricket matches on the green. As the Blunden family expanded (by 1910 there were nine children), they moved from the village schoolhouse to Congelow, a farmhouse in which Blunden discovered a cupboard full of his father's old books and magazines to supplement his reading. He explored the countryside by bicycle as he got older, little realising how his observational skills might be valued later:

> … these rides were delightful, for every crooked lane and smithy and timber-yard and country-box came before me in its individuality. That sense is gone nowadays. It stayed with me some years, even in the battlefields of Flanders, where generally I saw and

felt every communication trench and every sandbagged ruin as a personal, separate figure, quite distinct from every other one.[3]

Like his father, he took up cricket with a life-long passion.

It became obvious that he was outgrowing the village school, however, and it was suggested that he try for a scholarship to Christ's Hospital, a charitable school founded in 1552 which had recently moved its boy boarders from London to Horsham, in the middle of the Sussex Weald. The pupils' Tudor uniforms of yellow stockings, blue breeches and long blue coats gave rise to the name 'Old Blues' for alumni, amongst whom were Samuel Taylor Coleridge, Leigh Hunt and Charles Lamb. Blunden arrived, with some trepidation, in 1909. 'Forefathers', published in 1920 (p.23), evokes the village world he left behind, and its 'unrecorded, unrenowned' inhabitants. While entry to Christ's Hospital was predicated on 'honest origin and poverty',[4] Blunden was moving into a world of greater sophistication, into a tradition of record and renown. He became passionately attached to the school and its literary traditions, and flourished there. If his schooling set him apart from his family and their mixed fortunes, it did not alter his devotion to the Kent of his childhood, as he later wrote in 'The Deeper Friendship' (p.92):

Were all eyes changed, were even poetry cold,
Were those long systems of hope that I tried to deploy
Skeletons, still I should keep one final hold,
Since clearer and clearer returns my first-found joy.

This deep-seated love of the countryside was the wellspring of much of his poetry, and it was expressed in close observation of wildlife and landscape: 'The rose-finned roach and bluish bream / And staring ruffe steal up the stream'; on a November morning 'The rooks with terror's tumult take their rounds, / Under the eaves the chattering sparrows pine'; in 'Cloudy June', 'nightjars burr and yapping fox steps by / And hedgehogs wheeze and play in glimmering brown'; he could recall at will the sight of 'the hill's hopgrounds to the lowest leas / In the rook-routed vale'. It made him deeply receptive to the poetry of John Clare, which he discovered as a schoolboy and was later to help bring back to notice; it also fostered a taste for eighteenth-century poets such as William Collins and Thomas Gray. A real countryman's knowledge, including an ear for the dialects of Kent and Sussex, and wide reading was enriched by a sensitivity to spiritual experience, underpinned by a boyhood in the church choir and familiarity with the King James Bible.

He loved Shelley, and Henry Vaughan – his last literary pilgrimage included a visit to Vaughan's grave – and there are poems in tribute to all these forebears scattered throughout his work, as well as scholarly articles, reviews and editions. It is perhaps difficult for us now to understand how such formative influences might work on an adolescent boy: a patriotism of land and language, a combination of eighteenth-century decorum and romantic yearning, country skills and scholastic pleasures. So that what seems to a modern reader artificial, archaic, or sentimental – and there are these strains in Blunden's work – was the result of a deeply literary sensibility working over an experience of extraordinary historical continuity.

> The reign of King Edward seemed [...] a golden security. Everything did: the *Daily Telegraph*, the fishmonger at his due hour [...], the flower show, and the never-delayed 2.23 to Maidstone on Saturday afternoon. The ripened apple-orchards and the light smoke from the September hop-kilns were always there.[5]

His skills and passions were all in place by 1914, when this apparently stable world was inexorably altered. Blunden completed his schooling, and cycled over to join the Royal Sussex Regiment in August 1915. He was supposed to be taking up a scholarship in Classics at The Queen's College, Oxford. Instead, aged 19, he was shortly to find himself en route to the Somme: 'shellholes, telegraph wires in hanks, rusty ruins of factories, gunpits, a forbidding loneliness, the canal like green glue, stagnant and stinking.'[6]

He had already started writing and privately publishing poetry. One of the many incongruous scenes in his classic memoir, *Undertones of War* (never out of print since its publication in 1928), is that of his commanding officer asking him to dinner with the officers on the strength of a good review of *Pastorals* in the *Times Literary Supplement*; he was 'overjoyed at having an actual author in his battalion'.[7] Blunden was known as 'Rabbit' – shy, endearing, a fast runner – in those killing fields; elsewhere, he was often compared to a bird, even down to the graceful trace of his handwriting.[8]

Blunden was at the Front longer than any other of the war poets, surviving the Somme and Passchendaele. Memories and nightmares remained with him to the end of his life, along with breathing problems and escape through alcohol: now he would be diagnosed as suffering from post-traumatic stress disorder. He tried Oxford, but like many returned servicemen could not settle into the path he had been expected to follow. In 1918 he had married Mary Daines, and their first child had died aged five weeks in 1919. They went on to have two more – Clare and John – but the family did not accompany him when, to improve their financial situation, he took up the post of Professor of English at the Imperial University of Tokyo.[9] There were already difficulties in the marriage, predictable perhaps because of their youth and very different experiences, and Blunden's burgeoning literary career and friendships with which Mary mainly felt uncomfortable. Sassoon was an exception. Blunden had met Sassoon in 1919 and they maintained a close friendship and voluminous correspondence; Sassoon also supported him through periods of financial difficulty. While they shared passions for book collecting, cricket and Kent, their war experience was the cementing factor.

Lonely in Japan, Blunden writes in his 1926 essay 'War and Peace': 'And if this winter is not contrary to the last, I shall often seem to be in Flanders, while the smoky gloom of dull weather gloats upon the dark unfruiting clay…' – 'unfruiting' is typical of the negative prepositions that crop up in the poems, perhaps showing the influence of Thomas Hardy.

> The war itself with all its desperate drudgery is not the predominant part of these memories – I need a more intense word than Memories; it is Nature as then disclosed by fits and starts, as then most luckily encountered 'in spite of sorrow', that so occupies me still.[10]

This is an expression of the deep contradiction at work in his poetry and prose: that such remembrance is both confining and enlarging. It does not let Blunden go, and at some level he does not want it to, because it provides reminders of solace and comrades to whom he remains unswervingly loyal. Yet, as Marlowe wrote, 'this is Hell, nor am I out of it'. Charles Carrington, Blunden's exact contemporary and also a Somme veteran, put it brutally: 'I could not escape from the comradeship of the trenches which had become a mental internment camp.'[11]

What could Nature provide in the way of solace or security when the identities of soldier and civilian blurred? Blunden was too keen an observer, too sophisticated a writer, to see a simple opposition between the war as machine and the garden as paradise. Indeed some of his best-known poems – 'The Pike' (p.11) , for example, and 'The Midnight Skaters' (p.67) – show how destruction and death shadow even the peaceable pastimes of angling and skating, and martial vocabulary detonates in countryside scenes. Yet woods, streams, flowers and birds do provide elements of unchanging pleasure, and in 'Old Homes' (*English Poems*, 1925) Blunden returns to the vision of Yalding as sacred ground and talisman:

> Beyond estranging years that cloaked my view
> With all their wintriness of fear and strain;
> I turned to you, I never turned in vain.

Blunden did make friends in Japan, slowly; his students were devoted to him, and he had an affair with a student teacher seven years his senior, Aki Hayashi. She followed him to England when he resumed the ups and downs of married life there in 1927. Love on his part turned to loyalty and such material support as he was able to give; her complete and lonely devotion was life-long. He returned to literary journalism at the same exhausting rate of production he had maintained before the Japanese interlude, contributing 400 essays and reviews to journals over about three years, as well as editions of various poets' works. Blunden's edition of *The Poems of Wilfred Owen* was published in 1931, the same year that his marriage formally ended. The Owen volume supplanted Siegfried Sassoon's earlier edition, and was to remain standard for many years: a work of scholarship, it was also a tribute to a comrade in arms.

When Blunden later wrote a pamphlet about the war poets, he picked out 'The Show' as evidencing Owen's 'spiritual and mental dignity' in its 'unveiling of a stupendous, automatic, painful scene of modern war – almost the hieroglyph of the end... of our civilisation'; he also remarked on Owen's 'deeply considered technique' which 'was part of the offering that this soldier poet made to eventual peace and mercy.'[12] The 'poetical supplement' to *Undertones of War*, and the war poems that continued to seed themselves through subsequent volumes – 'Premature Rejoicing' (p.98), 'November 1, 1931' (p.111), 'The Lost Battalion' (p.114), 'On a Picture by Dürer' (p.123) are just a few – can also be seen in this light. The 'considered technique' of Blunden's poetry in general, ranging from conversation piece to monologue, sonnet to ballad, from the double-accented metrical simplicity of 'The Puzzle' (p.68) to the intricate modulations of 'Late

Light' (p.118), is one aspect of his attempt at controlling his experience, but also expresses a continuity with preceding literary tradition that might extend a bridge into the age of peace.

Like two other outstanding Great War writers, Ivor Gurney (whose poems Blunden edited for publication in 1954 at the composer Gerald Finzi's urging) and David Jones (who served almost as long at the Front as Blunden), surviving the war involved 'going over the ground again', as he writes in 'Another Journey from Béthune to Cuinchy' (p.81). In Blunden's case this was also literal, as he was appointed Kipling's successor on the Imperial War Graves Commission. The remembrance of war continued to make him an uneasy tenant of such peace as the 1930s provided. There was a certain stability in his new position as Fellow and Tutor in English at Merton College, Oxford, and in a new marriage with the writer Sylva Norman in 1933. He published a collection of 300 poems, *Poems 1914–1930*, at the beginning of the decade, followed by more volumes of poems and essays; he gave the Clark Lectures at Cambridge, on Charles Lamb and his contemporaries. He was established as the author of *Undertones*, which went into eight impressions in two years. Sassoon wrote to him: 'You and I are popular prose-men now, but let us always remember that Poetry is our heavenly spouse.'[13]

After the gradual ending of his marriage to Sylva Norman, who did not share his desire for family life, Blunden left Merton to become a staff writer on the *Times Literary Supplement*. His third marriage, to his student Claire Poynting, a lover of literature and cricket, was celebrated as the Second World War ended in 1945. It brought him great happiness: 'she is like some clear horizon, like my first view of the sea coast as a child, a better light and day', he wrote in his diary.[14] After the war, Blunden returned to Japan for two years as a Cultural Liaison Officer, accompanied by his wife and young child. His students and audiences were respectful and welcoming, and he undertook a demanding schedule of work there. While 'A Japanese Evening' (p.99) hints at barriers to understanding, it registers a discretely sensuous awareness of another culture. Blunden found much that was sympathetic in the 'beautiful and dexterous and delicate detail of existence' in Japanese art,[15] and the tranquil austerity of the sacred places he visited.

Reverting to the precarious world of literary journalism was not ideal for a man with a growing family – there were four daughters by 1956 – and so in 1953 Blunden became Professor of English at the

University of Hong Kong. He was notably generous with his time and scholarship to students and colleagues. He writes to Sassoon of visitors passing through Hong Kong such as Vera Brittain, Graham Greene, and the cricketer John Arlott, whom he received with pleasure. The poems of these hardworking years abroad draw on his memories of Kent and Sussex, as well as describing his domestic surroundings, as in 'A Hong Kong House' (p.144) and the poignant sonnet 'Dog on Wheels' (p.146). Blunden relished the antics of flies and birds, marked the death of snail and mouse, 'All tenants of an ancient place' as Clare wrote; like him, Blunden was always ready to give '"every weed and blossom" an equality with whatever this world contains'.[16]

He had been made CBE in 1951, and in 1956 was awarded the Queen's Gold Medal for Poetry. Yet as his biographer Barry Webb makes clear, these were years of strain below the surface of achievements and lively family life. He was conscious of failing physically and poetically, and the combination was destructive of any peace of mind, as were the recurrent war dreams. He gradually lost the war comrades who had meant so much to him; Annie, the German sister-in-law he had loved; Aki Hayashi; and Gerald Finzi, who had set his poems to music. It was time to go home.

Blunden retired to Long Melford, Suffolk, in 1964. He continued to lecture, to write (less and less poetry), to visit northern France and Flanders. Two years later he was elected Professor of Poetry at Oxford; ironically, as Webb notes, given a public platform at the time he was least confident to mount it.[17] He stepped down for health reasons in 1968, a year after the death of his 100-year-old mother and of Sassoon,[18] and died at Long Melford in 1974. His headstone in the village churchyard is engraved with words from his poem 'Seers', modest to the end: 'I live still, to love still / Things quiet and unconcerned.'

Blunden wrote to his student Keith Douglas, the poet who was to die in Normandy in 1944, that 'the fighting man in this as in other wars is at least the only man whom truth really cares to meet.'[19] This conviction, shared by many subsequent critics, has perhaps helped to obscure Blunden's achievements. Readers of First World War poets think of them as 'fighting men', writing from the muddy trenches, their poetry essentially validated by that experience. What if a poet's truth is survival, and all that carries of guilt, of acute sensitivity to loveliness as well as loss? For Blunden, literature – its making and its long tradition of makers – is a chief part of what steadies the poet in an inherently unsteady world, along with deep roots in English country life. He offers us his perceptions, consolations, devastations as a poet of remembrance whose witness needs revaluation; whose poems throw their long shadows and moments of illumination far beyond this centenary year of 2018.

Robyn Marsack

A NOTE ON THE TEXT

The poems are mainly printed in the order of their first publication in collections; where this varies it is noted, along with significant changes to poems in subsequent editions. For the poems connected with *Undertones of War*, interested readers should consult John Greening's edition, where changes in words and punctuation have been scrupulously annotated. (References to *Undertones* here have been given by chapter not page, as several editions of the book are available.) Pre-1920 poems are dated where possible, from a variety of printed and manuscript sources; Martin Taylor's selection of Blunden's war poems, *Overtones of War* (London: Gerald Duckworth & Co, 1996), has been most useful. Dates without square brackets are as printed in the collections.

Acknowledgements

Material from the annotated version of *Edmund Blunden's Poems 1914–1930* quoted in the notes is published by permission of the Harry Ransom Center The University of Texas at Austin. I appreciated Elizabeth Garver's assistance in obtaining this.

I am grateful to the Royal Literary Fund for a Writing Fellowship at the University of Glasgow during the making of this edition, and for the access that gave me to the resources of the University Library.

My warmest thanks to Madeleine Airlie, for her direction to texts on trauma; John Greening for his advice; Diana Hendry for her support; Edna Longley for her insight and comments; Jonathan Meuli for his copy-editing and proofing; and especially to Margi Blunden, whose knowledge and advocacy of her father's work is invaluable. I feel privileged to have had her insights to add to those of Claire Blunden, who was so encouraging when I undertook the first edition of EB's poems in 1982.

By Chanctonbury

We shuddered on the blotched and wrinkled down,
So gaunt and chilled with solitary breeze.
Sharp stubborn grass, black-heather trails, wild trees
Knotting their knared wood like a thorny crown –
Huge funnelled dips to chalklands streaked with brown,
White railway smoke-drills dimming by degrees,
Slow ploughs afield, flood waters on the leas,
And red roofs of the small, ungainly town:
And blue fog over all, and saddening all –
Thus lay the landscape. Up from the sea there loomed
A stately airship, clear and large awhile:
Then, gliding grandly inland many a mile,
It left our Druid height that black graves plumed,
Vanishing fog-like in the foggy pall.

The Festubert Shrine

A sycamore on either side
In whose lovely leafage cried
   Hushingly the little winds –
Thus was Mary's shrine descried.

'Sixteen Hundred and Twenty-Four'
Legended above the door,
   'Pray, sweet gracious Lady, pray
For our souls,'– and nothing more.

Builded of rude grey stones and these
Scarred and marred from base to frieze
   With the shrapnel's pounces – ah,
Fair she braved War's gaunt disease:

Fair she pondered on the strange
Embitterments of latter change,
   Looking fair towards Festubert,
Cloven roof and tortured grange.

Work of carving too there was,
(Once had been her reredos),
   In this cool and peaceful cell
That the hoarse guns blared across.

Twisted oaken pillars graced
With oaken amaranths interlaced
   In oaken garlandry, had borne
Her holy niche – and now laid waste.

Mary, pray for us? O pray!
In thy dwelling by this way
   What poor folks have knelt to thee!
We are no less poor than they.

May 1916

Thiepval Wood

The tired air groans as the heavies swing over, the river-hollows boom;
The shell-fountains leap from the swamps, and with wildfire and fume
      The shoulder of the chalkdown convulses.
Then jabbering echoes stampede in the slatting wood,
Ember-black the gibbet trees like bones or thorns protrude
      From the poisonous smoke – past all impulses.
To them these silvery dews can never again be dear,
Nor the blue javelin-flames of thunderous noons strike fear.

September 1916

'Transport Up' at Ypres

The thoroughfares that seem so dead to daylight passers-by
Change character when dark comes down, and traffic starts to ply;
Never a noisier street than the Boulevard Malou becomes
With the cartwheels jolting the dead awake, and the cars like
     rumbling drums.

The crazy houses watch them pass, and stammer with the roar,
The drivers hustle on their mules, more come behind and more;
Briskly the black mules clatter by, to-day was Devil's Mass;
The loathly smell of picric here, and there a touch of gas.

From silhouette to pitchy blur, beneath the bitter stars,
The interminable convoy streams of horses, vans, and cars.
They clamour through the cheerless night, the streets a slattern maze,
The sentries at the corners shout them on their different ways.

And so they go, night after night, and chance the shrapnel fire,
The sappers' waggons stowed with frames and concertina wire,
The ration-limbers for the line, the lorries for the guns:
While overhead with fleering light stare down those withered suns.

[January 1917]

Les Halles d'Ypres

A tangle of iron rods and spluttered beams,
   On brickwork past the skill of a mason to mend:
A wall with a bright blue poster – odd as dreams
   Is the city's latter end.

A shapeless obelisk looms Saint Martin's spire,
   Now a lean aiming-mark for the German guns;
And the Cloth Hall crouches beside, disfigured with fire,
   The glory of Flanders once.

Only the foursquare tower still bears the trace
   Of beauty that was, and strong embattled age,
And gilded ceremonies and pride of place –
   Before this senseless rage.

And still you may see (below the noon serene,
   The mysterious, changeless vault of sharp blue light),
The pigeons come to the tower, and flaunt and preen,
   And flicker in playful flight.

[January 1917]

Clear Weather

A cloudless day! with a keener line
    The ruins jut on the glintering blue,
The gas gongs by the billets shine
    Like gold or wine, so trim and new.

Sharp through the wreckage pries the gust,
    And down the roads where wheels have rolled
Whirls the dry snow in powdery dust,
    And starlings muster ruffled with cold.

The gunners profit by the light,
    The guns like surly yard-dogs bark;
And towards Saint Jean in puffs of white
    The anti-aircraft find a mark.

And now the sentries' whistles ply,
    For overhead with whirring drone
An Albatros comes racing by,
    Immensely high, and one of our own

From underneath to meet it mounts,
    And banks and spirals up, and straight
The popping maxims' leaden founts
    Spurt fire, the Boche drops like a weight:

A hundred feet he nose-dives, then
    He rights himself and scuds down sky
Towards the German lines again,
    A great transparent dragon-fly.

[Early 1917]

Trees on the Calais Road

Like mourners filing into church at a funeral,
    These droop their sombre heads and troop to the coast,
The untimely rain makes mystery round them all
    And the wind flies round them like the ghost
    That the body on the blackened trestles lost.

Miserere sobs the weary
Sky, sackclothed, stained, and dreary,
And they bend their heads and sigh
    Miserere, Miserere!

With natural dole and lamentation
They groan for the slaughter and desecration,
But every moment adds to the cry
Of that dead army driving by.

1917

Bleue Maison

Now to attune my dull soul, if I can,
To the contentment of this countryside
Where man is not forever killing man
But quiet days like these calm waters glide.
And I will praise the blue flax in the rye,
And pathway bindweed's trumpet-like attire,
Pink rest-harrow and curlock's glistening eye,
And poppies flaring like St Elmo's fire.

And I will praise the willow's silver-grey,
And where I stand the road is rippled over
With airy dreams of blossomed bean and clover,
And shyest birds come elfin-like to play:
And in the rifts of blue above the trees
Pass the full sails of natural Odysseys.

1917

Almswomen

for Nancy and Robert

At Quincey's moat the squandering village ends,
And there in the almshouse dwell the dearest friends
Of all the village, two old dames that cling
As close as any trueloves in the spring.
Long, long ago they passed threescore-and-ten,
And in this doll's house lived together then;
All things they have in common, being so poor,
And their one fear, Death's shadow at the door.
Each sundown makes them mournful, each sunrise
Brings back the brightness in their failing eyes.

How happy go the rich fair-weather days
When on the roadside folk stare in amaze
At such a honeycomb of fruit and flowers
As mellows round their threshold; what long hours
They gloat upon their steepling hollyhocks,
Bee's balsams, feathery southernwood, and stocks,
Fiery dragon's-mouths, great mallow leaves
For salves, and lemon-plants in bushy sheaves,
Shagged Esau's-hands with five green finger-tips.
Such old sweet names are ever on their lips.
As pleased as little children where these grow
In cobbled pattens and worn gowns they go,
Proud of their wisdom when on gooseberry shoots
They stuck eggshells to fright from coming fruits
The brisk-billed rascals; pausing still to see
Their neighbour owls saunter from tree to tree,
Or in the hushing half-light mouse the lane
Long-winged and lordly.
                      But when those hours wane,
Indoors they ponder, scared by the harsh storm
Whose pelting saracens on the window swarm,
And listen for the mail to clatter past
And church clock's deep bay withering on the blast;
They feed the fire that flings a freakish light
On pictured kings and queens grotesquely bright,

Platters and pitchers, faded calendars
And graceful hour-glass trim with lavenders.

Many a time they kiss and cry, and pray
That both be summoned in the self-same day,
And wiseman linnet tinkling in his cage
End too with them the friendship of old age,
And all together leave their treasured room
Some bell-like evening when the may's in bloom.

[1918]

The Pike

From shadows of rich oaks outpeer
The moss-green bastions of the weir,
Where the quick dipper forages
In elver-peopled crevices,
And a small runlet trickling down the sluice
Gossamer music tires not to unloose.

Else round the broad pool's hush
Nothing stirs,
Unless sometime a straggling heifer crush
Through the thronged spinney where the pheasant whirs;
Or martins in a flash
Come with wild mirth to dip their magical wings,
While in the shallow some doomed bulrush swings
At whose hid root the diver vole's teeth gnash.

And nigh this toppling reed, still as the dead
The great pike lies, the murderous patriarch
Watching the waterpit sheer-shelving dark,
Where through the plash his lithe bright vassals thread.

The rose-finned roach and bluish bream
And staring ruffe steal up the stream
Hard by their glutted tyrant, now
Still as a sunken bough.

He on the sandbank lies,
Sunning himself long hours
With stony gorgon eyes:
Westward the hot sun lowers.

Sudden the grey pike changes, and quivering poises for slaughter;
Intense terror wakens around him, the shoals scud awry, but
there chances
A chub unsuspecting; the prowling fins quicken, in fury he lances;
And the miller that opens the hatch stands amazed at the whirl in
the water.

1919

The Unchangeable

Though I within these two last years of grace
Have seen bright Ancre scourged to brackish mire,
And meagre Belgian becks by dale and chace
Stamped into sloughs of death with battering fire, –
Spite of all this, I sing you high and low,
My old loves, waters, be you shoal or deep,
Waters whose lazy and continual flow
Learns at the drizzling weir the tongue of sleep.

For Sussex cries from primrose lags and brakes,
'Why do you leave my woods untrod so long?
Still float the bronze carp on my lilied lakes,
Still the wood-fairies round my spring wells throng;
And chancing lights on willowy waterbreaks
Dance to the dabbling brooks' midsummer song.'

1917

A Waterpiece

The wild-rose bush lets loll
Her sweet-breathed petals on the pearl-smooth pool,
The bream-pool overshadowed with the cool
Of oaks where myriad mumbling wings patrol.

There the live dimness burrs with droning glees
Of hobby-horses with their starting eyes,
And violet humble-bees and dizzy flies;
That from the dewsprings drink the honeyed lees.

Up the slow stream the immemorial bream
(For when had Death dominion over them?)
Through green pavilions of ghost leaf and stem,
A conclave of blue shadows in a dream,
Glide on; idola that forgotten plan,
Incomparably wise, the doom of man.

1919

A Country God

When groping farms are lanterned up
    And stolchy ploughlands hid in grief,
And glimmering byroads catch the drop
    That weeps from sprawling twig and leaf,
And heavy-hearted spins the wind
    Among the tattered flags of Mirth, –
Then who but I flit to and fro,
With shuddering speech, with mope and mow,
    And glass the eyes of Earth?

Then haunt I by some moaning brook
    Where lank and snaky brambles swim
Or where the hill pines swartly look
    I whirry through the dark and hymn
A dull-voiced dirge and threnody,
    An echo of the world's sad drone
That now appals the friendly stars –
O wail for blind brave youth whose wars
    Turn happiness to stone.

How rang my cavern-shades of old
    To my melodious pipes, and then
My bright-haired bergomask patrolled
    Each lawn and plot for laughter's din:
Never a sower flung broadcast,
    No hedger brished nor scythesman swung,
Nor maiden trod the purpling press,
But I was by to guard and bless
    And for their solace sung.

★ ★ ★

But now the sower's hand is writhed
    In livid death, the bright rhythm stolen,
The gold grain flatted and unscythed,
    The boars in the vineyard, gnarled and sullen,
Havocking the grapes; and the pouncing wind
    Spins the spattered leaves of the glen
In a mockery dance, death's hue-and-cry;
With all my murmurous pipes flung by,
    And summer not to come again.

1918

In Festubert

Now everything that shadowy thought
    Lets peer with bedlam eyes at me
From alleyways and thoroughfares
    Of cynic and ill memory
Lifts a gaunt head, sullenly stares,
    Shuns me as a child has shunned
A hizzing dragonfly that daps
    Above his mudded pond.

Now bitter frosts, muffling the morn
    In old days, crunch the grass anew;
There, where the floods made fields forlorn
    The glinzy ice grows thicker through.
The pollards glower like mummies when
    Thieves pierce the long-locked pyramid,
Inscrutable as those dead men
    With painted mask and balm-cloth hid;

And all the old delight is cursed
    Redoubling present undelight.
Splinter, crystal, splinter and burst;
And sear no more with second sight.

1916

Perch-Fishing

For G. W. Palmer

On the far hill the cloud of thunder grew
And sunlight blurred below: but sultry blue
Burned yet on the valley water where it hoards
Behind the miller's elmen floodgate boards,
And there the wasps, that lodge them ill-concealed
In the vole's empty house, still drove afield
To plunder touchwood from old crippled trees
And build their young ones their hutched nurseries;
Still creaked the grasshoppers' rasping unison
Nor had the whisper through the tansies run
Nor weather-wisest bird gone home.
                                        How then
Should wry eels in the pebbled shallows ken
Lightning coming? troubled up they stole
To the deep-shadowed sullen water-hole,
Among whose warty snags the quaint perch lair.

As cunning stole the boy to angle there,
Muffling least tread, with no noise balancing through
The hangdog alder-boughs his bright bamboo.
Down plumbed the shuttled ledger, and the quill
On the quicksilver water lay dead still.

A sharp snatch, swirling to-fro of the line,
He's lost, he's won, with splash and scuffling shine
Past the low-lapping brandy-flowers drawn in,
The ogling hunchback perch with needled fin.
And there beside him one as large as he,
Following his hooked mate, careless who shall see
Or what befall him, close and closer yet –
The startled boy might take him in his net
That folds the other.
                        Slow, while on the clay
The other flounces, slow he sinks away.

What agony usurps that watery brain
For comradeship of twenty summers slain,
For such delights below the flashing weir
And up the sluice-cut, playing buccaneer
Among the minnows; lolling in hot sun
When bathing vagabonds had drest and done;
Rootling in salty flannel-weed for meal
And river-shrimps, when hushed the trundling wheel;
Snapping the dapping moth, and with new wonder
Prowling through old drowned barges falling asunder.
And O a thousand things the whole year through
They did together, never more to do.

1919

Malefactors

Nailed to these green laths long ago,
You cramp and shrivel into dross,
Blotched with mildews, gnawed with moss,
And now the eye can scarcely know
The snake among you from the kite –
   So sharp does Death's fang bite.

I guess your stories; you were shot
Hovering above the miller's chicks;
And you, coiled on his threshold bricks –
Hissing, you died; and you, Sir Stoat,
Dazzled with stableman's lantern stood
   And tasted crabtree wood.

Here then you leered-at luckless churls,
Clutched to your clumsy gibbet, shrink
To shapeless orts; hard by the brink
Of this black scowling pond that swirls
To turn the wheel beneath the mill,
   The wheel so long since still.

There's your revenge, the wheel at tether,
The miller gone, the white planks rotten,
The very name of the mill forgotten,
Dimness and silence met together…
Felons of fur and feather, can
   There lurk some crime in man –

In man your executioner,
Whom here Fate's cudgel battered down?
Did he too filch from squire and clown?…
The damp gust makes the ivy whir
Like passing death, the sluices well,
   Dreary as a passing-bell.

1919

Clare's Ghost

Pitch-dark night shuts in, and the rising gale
    Is full of the presage of rain,
    And there comes a withered wail
    From the wainscot and jarring pane,
    And a long funeral surge
    Like a wood-god's dirge,
Like the wash of the shoreward tides, from the firs on the crest.

The shaking hedges blacken, the last gold flag
    Lowers from the west;
The Advent bell moans wild like a witch hag
    In the storm's unrest,
And the lychgate lantern's candle weaves a shroud,
    And the unlatched gate shrieks loud.

Up fly the smithy sparks, but are baffled from soaring
    By the pelting scurry, and ever
As puff the bellows, a multitude more outpouring
    Die foiled in the endeavour;

And a stranger stands with me here in the glow
Chinked through the door, and marks
        The sparks
Perish in whirlpool wind, and if I go
To the delta of cypress, where the glebe gate cries,
I see him there, with his streaming hair
        And his eyes
Piercing beyond our human firmament,
Lit with a burning deathless discontent.

1917

11th R.S.R.

How bright a dove's wing shows against the sky
When thunder's blackening up in monstrous cloud;
How silver clear against war's hue and cry
Each syllable of peace the gods allowed!
Even common things in anguish have grown rare
As legends of a richer life gone by,
Like flowers that in their time are no one's care,
But blooming late are loved and grudged to die.

What mercy is it, that I live and move,
If haunted ever by war's agony?
Nature is love and will remember love,
And kindly uses those whom fear set free;
Let me not even think of you as dead,
O never dead! you live, your old songs yet
Pass me each day, your faith still routs my dread,
Your past and future are my parapet.

You looked before and after! these calm shires,
The doting sun, the orchards all aflame,
These joyful flocking swallows round the spires,
Bonfires and turreted stacks – well may you claim,
Still seeing these sweet familiar bygones, all!
Still dwells in you their has-been, their to-be,
And walking in their light you fear no fall.
This is your holding: mine, across the sea,

Where much I find to trace old friendship by:
'Here one bade us farewell,' 'Here supped we then,'
'Wit never sweeter fell than that July' –
Even sometimes comes the praise of better men.
The land lies like a jewel in the mind,
And featured sharp shall lie when other fades,
And through its veins the eternal memories wind
As that lost column down its colonnades.

Flat parcelled fields the scanty paths scored through,
Woods where no guns thrust their lean muzzles out,
Small smoky inns, we laughed at war's ado!
And clutching death, to hear, fell into doubt.
Christ at each crossroad hung, rich belfries tolling,
Old folks a-digging, weathercocks turned torches,
Half-hearted railways, flimsy millsails rolling –
Not one, but by the host for ever marches.

Forefathers

Here they went with smock and crook,
    Toiled in the sun, lolled in the shade,
Here they mudded out the brook
    And here their hatchet cleared the glade:
Harvest-supper woke their wit,
Huntsmen's moon their wooings lit.

From this church they led their brides,
    From this church themselves were led
Shoulder-high; on these waysides
    Sat to take their beer and bread.
Names are gone – what men they were
These their cottages declare.

Names are vanished, save the few
    In the old brown Bible scrawled;
These were men of pith and thew,
    Whom the city never called;
Scarce could read or hold a quill,
Built the barn, the forge, the mill.

On the green they watched their sons
    Playing till too dark to see,
As their fathers watched them once,
    As my father once watched me;
While the bat and beetle flew
On the warm air webbed with dew.

Unrecorded, unrenowned,
    Men from whom my ways begin,
Here I know you by your ground
    But I know you not within –
All is mist, and there survives
Not a moment of your lives.

Like the bee that now is blown
    Honey-heavy on my hand,
From his toppling tansy-throne
    In the green tempestuous land, –
I'm in clover now, nor know
Who made honey long ago.

November Morning

From the night storm sad wakes the winter day
With sobbings round the yew, and far-off surge
Of broadcast rain; the old house cries dismay,
And rising floods gleam silver on the verge
Of sackclothed skies and melancholy grounds.
On the black hop-pole slats the weazen bine,
The rooks with terror's tumult take their rounds,
Under the eaves the chattering sparrows pine.

Waked by the bald light from his bed of straw,
The beggar shudders out to steal and gnaw
Sheep's locusts: leaves the last of many homes –
Where mouldered apples and black shoddy lie,
Hop-shovels spluttered, wickered flasks flung by,
And sharded pots and rusty curry combs.

Spring Night

Through the smothered air the wicker finds
A muttering voice, 'crick' cries the embered ash,
Sharp rains knap at the panes beyond the blinds,
The flues and eaves moan, the jarred windows clash;
And like a sea breaking its barriers, flooding
New green abysses with untold uproar,
The cataract nightwind whelms the time of budding,
Swooping in sightless fury off the moor
Into our valley. Not a star shines. Who
Would guess the martin and the cuckoo come,
The pear in bloom, the bloom gone from the plum,
The cowslips countless as a morning dew?
So mad it blows, so truceless and so grim,
As if day's host of flowers were a moment's whim.

Sheet Lightning

When on the green the rag-tag game had stopt
And red the lights through alehouse curtains glowed,
The clambering brake drove out and took the road.
Then on the stern moors all the babble dropt
Among those merry men, who felt the dew
Sweet to the soul and saw the southern blue
Thronged with heat lightning miles and miles abroad,
Working and whickering, snakish, winged and clawed,
Or like an old carp lazily rising and shouldering.
Long the slate cloud flank shook with the death-white smouldering:
Yet not a voice.
           The night drooped oven-hot;
Then where the turnpike pierced the black wood plot,
Tongues wagged again and each man felt the grim
Destiny of the hour speak through him,
And then tales came of dwarfs on Starling Hill
And those young swimmers drowned at the roller Mill,
Where on the drowsiest noon an undertow
Famishing for life boiled like a pot below:
And how two higglers at the Walnut Tree
Had curst the Lord in thunderstorm and He
Had struck them dead as soot with lightning then –
It left the tankards whole, it chose the men.
Many a lad and many a lass was named
Who once stept bold and proud; but death had tamed
Their revel on the eve of May; cut short
The primrosing and promise of good sport,
Shut up the score book, laid the ribbands by.

Such bodings mustered from the fevered sky;
But now the spring well through the honeycomb
Of scored stone rumbling tokened them near home,
The whip-lash clacked, the jog-trot sharpened, all
Sang Farmer's Boy as loud as they could bawl,
And at the Walnut Tree the homeward brake
Stopt for hoarse ribaldry to brag and slake.

The weary wildfire faded from the dark;
While this one damned the parson, that the clerk;
And anger's balefire forked from the unbared blade
At word of things gone wrong or stakes not paid:

While Joe the driver stooped with oath to find
A young jack rabbit in the roadway, blind
Or dazzled by the lamps, as stiff as steel
With fear. Joe beat its brains out on the wheel.

Cloudy June

Above the hedge the spearman thistle towers
And thinks himself the god of all he sees;
But nettles jostle fearless where he glowers,
Like old and stained and sullen tapestries;
And elbowing hemlocks almost turn to trees,
Proud as the sweetbriar with her bubble flowers,
    Where puft green spider cowers
    To trap the toiling bees.

Here joy shall muse what melancholy tells,
And melancholy smile because of joy,
Whether the poppy breathe arabian spells
To make them friends, or whistling gipsy-boy
Sound them a truce that nothing comes to cloy.
No sunray burns through this slow cloud, nor swells
    Noise save the browsing-bells,
    Half sorrow and half joy.

Night comes; from fens where blind grey castles frown
A veiled moon ventures on the cavernous sky,
No stir, no tassel-tremble on the down:
Mood dims to nothing: atom-like I lie
Where nightjars burr and yapping fox steps by
And hedgehogs wheeze and play in glimmering brown;
    And my swooned passions drown,
    Nor tell me I am I.

Mole Catcher

With coat like any mole's, as soft and black,
And hazel bows bundled beneath his arm,
With long-helved spade and rush bag on his back,
The trapper plods alone about the farm
And spies new mounds in the ripe pasture-land,
And where the lob-worms writhe up in alarm
And easy sinks the spade, he takes his stand
Knowing the moles' dark highroad runs below:
Then sharp and square he chops the turf, and day
Gloats on the opened turnpike through the clay.

Out from his wallet hurry pin and prong,
And trap, and noose to tie it to the bow;
And then his grand arcanum, oily and strong,
Found out by his forefather years ago
To scent the peg and witch the moles along.
The bow is earthed and arched ready to shoot
And snatch the death-knot fast round the first mole
Who comes and snuffs well pleased and tries to root
Past the sly nose peg; back again is put
The mould, and death left smirking in the hole.
The old man goes and tallies all his snares
And finds the prisoners there and takes his toll.

And moles to him are only moles; but hares
See him afield and scarcely cease to nip
Their dinners, for he harms not them; he spares
The drowning fly that of his ale would sip
And throws the ant the crumbs of comradeship.
And every time he comes into his yard
Grey linnet knows he brings the groundsel sheaf,
And clatters round the cage to be unbarred,
And on his finger whistles twice as hard. –
What his old vicar says, is his belief,
In the side pew he sits and hears the truth
And never misses once to ring his bell
On Sundays night and morn, nor once since youth
Has heard the chimes afield, but has heard tell
There's not a peal in England sounds so well.

The Scythe Struck by Lightning

A thick hot haze had choked the valley grounds
Long since, the dogday sun had gone his rounds
Like a dull coal half lit with sulky heat;
And leas were iron, ponds were clay, fierce beat
The blackening flies round moody cattle's eyes.
Wasps on the mudbanks seemed a hornet's size
That on the dead roach battened. The plough's increase
Stood under a curse.
              Behold, the far release!
Old wisdom breathless at her cottage door
'Sounds of abundance' mused, and heard the roar
Of marshalled armies in the silent air,
And thought Elisha stood beside her there,
And clacking reckoned ere the next nightfall
She'd turn the looking-glasses to the wall.

Faster than armies out of the burnt void
The hourglass clouds innumerably deployed,
And when the hay-folks next look up, the sky
Sags black above them; scarce is time to fly.
And most run for their cottages; but Ward,
The mower for the inn beside the ford,
And slow strides he with shouldered scythe still bare,
While to the coverts leaps the great-eyed hare.

As he came in the dust snatched up and whirled
Hung high, and like a bell-rope whipped and twirled;
The brazen light glared round, the haze resolved
Into demoniac shapes bulged and convolved.
Well might poor ewes afar make bleatings wild,
Though this old trusting mower sat and smiled,
For from the hush of many days the land
Had waked itself: and now on every hand
Shrill swift alarm-notes, cries and counter-cries,
Lowings and crowings came and throbbing sighs.
Now atom lightning brandished on the moor,
Then out of sullen drumming came the roar
Of thunder joining battle east and west:

In hedge and orchard small birds durst not rest,
Flittering like dead leaves and like wisps of straws,
And the cuckoo called again, for without pause
Oncoming voices in the vortex burred.
The storm came toppling like a wave, and blurred
In grey the trees that like black steeples towered.
The sun's last yellow died. Then who but cowered?
Down ruddying darkness floods the hideous flash,
And pole to pole the cataract whirlwinds clash.

Alone within the tavern parlour still
Sat the grey mower, pondering his God's will,
And flinching not to flame or bolt, that swooped
With a great hissing rain till terror drooped
In weariness: and then there came a roar
Ten-thousand-fold, he saw not, was no more –
But life bursts on him once again, and blood
Beats droning round, and light comes in a flood.

He stares and sees the sashes battered awry,
The wainscot shivered, the crocks shattered, and nigh,
His twisted scythe, melted by its fierce foe,
Whose Parthian shot struck down the chimney. Slow
Old Ward lays hand to his old working-friend,
And thanking God Whose mercy did defend
His servant, yet must drop a tear or two
And think of times when that old scythe was new;
And stands in silent grief, nor hears the voices
Of many a bird that through the land rejoices,
Nor sees through the smashed panes the seagreen sky,
That ripens into blue, nor knows the storm is by.

The Poor Man's Pig

Already fallen plum-bloom stars the green,
   And apple-boughs as knarred as old toads' backs
Wear their small roses ere a rose is seen;
   The building thrush watches old Job who stacks
The bright-peeled osiers on the sunny fence,
   The pent sow grunts to hear him stumping by,
And tries to push the bolt and scamper thence,
   But her ringed snout still keeps her to the sty.

Then out he lets her run; away she snorts
   In bundling gallop for the cottage door,
With hungry hubbub begging crusts and orts,
   Then like the whirlwind bumping round once more;
Nuzzling the dog, making the pullets run,
And sulky as a child when her play's done.

Behind the Line

Treasure not so the forlorn days
When dun clouds flooded the naked plains
    With foul remorseless rains;
    Tread not those memory ways
Where by the dripping alien farms,
Starved orchards with their shrivelled arms,
The bitter mouldering wind would whine
At the brisk mules clattering towards the Line.

Remember not with so sharp skill
Each chasm in the clouds that with strange fire
    Lit pyramid-fosse and spire
    Miles and miles from our hill;
In the magic glass, aye, then their lure
Like heaven's houses gleaming pure
Might soothe the long-imprisoned sight
And put the seething storm to flight.

Enact not you so like a wheel
The round of evenings in sandbagged rooms
    Where candles flicked the glooms;
    The jests old time could steal
From ugly destiny, on whose brink
The poor fools grappled fear with drink,
And snubbed the hungry raving guns
With endless tunes on gramophones.

About you spreads the world anew,
The old fields for all your sense rejoice,
    Music has found her ancient voice,
    From the hills there's heaven on earth to view;
And kindly Mirth will raise his glass
With you to bid dull Care go pass –
And still you wander muttering on
Over the shades of shadows gone.

Reunion in War

The windmill in his smock of white
    Stared from his little crest,
Like a slow smoke was the moonlight
    As I went like one possessed

Where the glebe path makes shortest way;
    The stammering wicket swung.
I passed amid the crosses grey
    Where opiate yew-boughs hung.

The bleached grass shuddered into sighs,
    The dogs that knew this moon
Far up were harrying sheep, the cries
    Of hunting owls went on.

And I among the dead made haste
    And over flat vault stones
Set in the path unheeding paced
    Nor thought of those chill bones.

Thus to my sweetheart's cottage I,
    Who long had been away,
Turned as the traveller turns adry
    To brooks to moist his clay.

Her cottage stood like a dream, so clear
    And yet so dark; and now
I thought to find my more than dear
    And if she'd kept her vow.

Old house-dog from his barrel came
    Without a voice, and knew
And licked my hand; all seemed the same
    To the moonlight and the dew.

By the white damson then I took
  The tallest osier wand
And thrice upon her casement strook,
  And she, so fair, so fond,

Looked out, and saw in wild delight
  And tiptoed down to me,
And cried in silent joy that night
  Beside the bullace tree.

O cruel time to take away,
  Or worse to bring agen;
Why slept not I in Flanders clay
  With all the murdered men?

For I had changed, or she had changed,
  Though true loves both had been,
Even while we kissed we stood estranged
  With the ghosts of war between.

We had not met but a moment ere
  War baffled joy, and cried,
'Love's but a madness, a burnt flare;
  The shell's a madman's bride.'

The cottage stood, poor stone and wood,
  Poorer than stone stood I;
Then from her kind arms moved in a mood
  As grey as the cereclothed sky.

The roosts were stirred, each little bird
  Called fearfully out for day;
The church clock with his dead voice whirred
  As if he bade me stay

To trace with madman's fingers all
  The letters on the stones
Where thick beneath the twitch roots crawl
  In dead men's envied bones.

A Farm near Zillebeke

Black clouds hide the moon, the amazement is gone;
The morning will come in weeping and rain;
The Line is all hushed – on a sudden anon
The fool bullets clack and guns mouth again.
I stood in the yard of a house that must die,
And still the black hame was stacked by the door,
And harness still hung there, and the dray waited by.

Black clouds hid the moon, tears blinded me more.

Festubert, 1916 [1916 Seen from 1921]

Tired with dull grief, grown old before my day,
I sit in solitude and only hear
Long silent laughters, murmurings of dismay,
The lost intensities of hope and fear;
In those old marshes yet the rifles lie,
On the thin breastwork flutter the grey rags,
The very books I read are there – and I
Dead as the men I loved, wait while life drags

Its wounded length from those sad streets of war
Into green places here, that were my own;
But now what once was mine is mine no more,
I look for such friends here and I find none.
With such strong gentleness and tireless will
Those ruined houses seared themselves in me,
Passionate I look for their dumb story still,
And the charred stub outspeaks the living tree.

I rise up at the singing of a bird
And scarcely knowing slink along the lane,
I dare not give a soul a look or word
For all have homes and none's at home in vain:
Deep red the rose burned in the grim redoubt,
The self-sown wheat around was like a flood,
In the hot path the lizards lolled time out,
The saints in broken shrines were bright as blood.

Sweet Mary's shrine between the sycamores!
There we would go, my friend of friends and I,
And snatch long moments from the grudging wars;
Whose dark made light intense to see them by …
Shrewd bit the morning fog, the whining shots
Spun from the wrangling wire; then in warm swoon
The sun hushed all but the cool orchard plots,
We crept in the tall grass and slept till noon.

Third Ypres: a Reminiscence

Triumph! How strange, how strong had triumph come
On weary hate of foul and endless war
When from its grey gravecloths awoke anew
The summer day. Among the tumbled wreck
Of fascined lines and mounds the light was peering,
Half-smiling upon us, and our newfound pride;
The terror of the waiting night outlived,
The time too crowded for the heart to count
All the sharp cost in friends killed on the assault.
No sap of all the octopus had held us,
Here stood we trampling down the ancient tyrant.
So shouting dug we among the monstrous pits.

Amazing quiet fell upon the waste,
Quiet intolerable to those who felt
The hurrying batteries beyond the masking hills
For their new parley setting themselves in array
In crafty fourms unmapped.
                                        No, these, smiled faith,
Are dumb for the reason of their overthrow.
They move not back, they lie among the crews
Twisted and choked, they'll never speak again.
Only the copse where once might stand a shrine
Still clacked and suddenly hissed its bullets by.

The War would end, the Line was on the move,
And at a bound the impassable was passed.
We lay and waited with extravagant joy.

Now dulls the day and chills; comes there no word
From those who swept through our new lines to flood
The lines beyond? but little comes, and so
Sure as a runner time himself's accosted.
And the slow moments shake their heavy heads,
And croak, 'They're done, they'll none of them get through.'
They're done, they've all died on the entanglements,
The wire stood up like an unplashed hedge and thorned
With giant spikes – and there they've paid the bill.

Then comes the black assurance, then the sky's
Mute misery lapses into trickling rain,
That wreathes and swims and soon shuts in our world.
And those distorted guns, that lay past use,
Why – miracles not over! – all a firing,
The rain's no cloak from their sharp eyes. And you,
Poor signaller, you I passed by this emplacement,
You whom I warned, poor dare-devil, waving your flags,
Among this screeching I pass you again and shudder
At the lean green flies upon the red flesh madding.
Runner, stand by a second. Your message. – He's gone,
Falls on a knee, and his right hand uplifted
Claws his last message from his ghostly enemy,
Turns stone-like. Well I liked him, that young runner,
But there's no time for that. O now for the word
To order us flash from these drowning roaring traps
And even hurl upon that snarling wire?
Why are our guns so impotent?

                              The grey rain,
Steady as the sand in an hourglass on this day,
Where through the window the red lilac looks,
And all's so still, the chair's odd click is noise –
The rain is all heaven's answer, and with hearts
Past reckoning we are carried into night
And even sleep is nodding here and there.

The second night steals through the shrouding rain.
We in our numb thought crouching long have lost
The mockery triumph, and in every runner
Have urged the mind's eye see the triumph to come,
The sweet relief, the straggling out of hell
Into whatever burrows may be given
For life's recall. Then the fierce destiny speaks.
This was the calm, we shall look back for this.
The hour is come; come, move to the relief!
Dizzy we pass the mule-strewn track where once
The ploughman whistled as he loosed his team;
And where he turned home-hungry on the road,
The leaning pollard marks us hungrier turning,

We crawl to save the remnant who have torn
Back from the tentacled wire, those whom no shell
Has charred into black carcasses – Relief!
They grate their teeth until we take their room,
And through the churn of moonless night and mud
And flaming burst and sour gas we are huddled
Into the ditches where they bawl sense awake
And in a frenzy that none could reason calm,
(Whimpering some, and calling on the dead)
They turn away: as in a dream they find
Strength in their feet to bear back that strange whim
Their body.

                     At the noon of the dreadful day
Our trench and death's is on a sudden stormed
With huge and shattering salvoes, the clay dances
In founts of clods around the concrete sties,
Where still the brain devises some last armour
To live out the poor limbs.

                       This wrath's oncoming
Found four of us together in a pillbox,
Skirting the abyss of madness with light phrases,
White and blinking, in false smiles grimacing.
The demon grins to see the game, a moment
Passes, and – still the drum-tap dongs my brain
To a whirring void – through the great breach above me
The light comes in with icy shock and the rain
Horridly drips. Doctor, talk, talk! if dead
Or stunned I know not; the stinking powdered concrete,
The lyddite turns me sick – my hair's all full
Of this smashed concrete. O I'll drag you, friends,
Out of the sepulchre into the light of day,
For this is day, the pure and sacred day.
And while I squeak and gibber over you,
Look, from the wreck a score of field-mice nimble,
And tame and curious look about them. (These
Calmed me, on these depended my salvation.)

There comes my sergeant, and by all the powers
The wire is holding to the right battalion,
And I can speak – but I myself first spoken
Hear a known voice now measured even to madness
Call me by name: 'For God's sake send and help us,
Here in a gunpit, all headquarters done for,
Forty or more, the nine-inch came right through.
All splashed with arms and legs, and I myself
The only one not killed, not even wounded.
You'll send – God bless you!' The more monstrous fate
Shadows our own, the mind swoons doubly burdened,
Taught how for miles our anguish groans and bleeds,
A whole sweet countryside amuck with murder;
Each moment puffed into a year with death.

Still wept the rain, roared guns,
Still swooped into the swamps of flesh and blood,
All to the drabness of uncreation sunk,
And all thought dwindled to a moan, – Relieve!
But who with what command can now relieve
The dead men from that chaos, or my soul?

Death of Childhood Beliefs

There the puddled lonely lane,
    Lost among the red swamp sallows,
Gleams through drifts of summer rain
    Down to ford the sandy shallows,
Where the dewberry brambles crane.

And the stream in cloven clay
    Round the bridging sheep-gate stutters,
Wind-spun leaves burn silver-grey,
    Far and wide the blue moth flutters
Over swathes of warm new hay.

Scrambling boys with mad to-do
    Paddle in the sedges' hem,
Ever finding joy anew;
    Clocks toll time out – not for them,
With what years to frolic through!

How shall I return and how
    Look once more on those old places!
For Time's cloud is on me now
    That each day, each hour effaces
Visions once on every bough.

Stones could talk together then,
    Jewels lay for hoes to find,
Each oak hid King Charles agen,
    Ay, nations in his powdered rind;
Sorcery lived with homeless men.

Spider Dick, with cat's green eyes
    That could pierce stone walls, has flitted –
By some hedge he shakes and cries,
    A lost man, half-starved, half-witted,
Whom the very stoats despise.

Trees on hill-tops then were Palms,
  Closing pilgrims' arbours in;
David walked there singing Psalms;
  Out of the clouds white seraphin
Leaned to watch us fill our bin.

Where's the woodman now to tell
  Will o' the Wisp's odd fiery anger?
Where's the ghost to toll the bell
  Startling midnight with its clangour
Till the wind seemed but a knell?

Drummers jumping from the tombs
  Banged and thumped all through the town,
Past shut shops and silent rooms
  While the flaming spires fell down; –
Now but dreary thunder booms.

Smuggler trapped in headlong spate,
  Smuggler's mare with choking whinney,
Well I knew your fame, your fate;
  By the ford and shaking spinney
Where you perished I would wait,

Half in glory, half in fear,
  While the fierce flood, trough and crest,
Whirled away the shepherd's gear,
  And sunset wildfire coursed the west,
Crying Armageddon near.

The Canal

Where so dark and still
Slept the water, never changing,
From the glad sport in the meadows
    Oft I turned me.

    Fear would strike me chill
On the clearest day in summer,
Yet I loved to stand and ponder
    Hours together

    By the tarred bridge rail –
There the lockman's vine-clad window,
Mirrored in the tomb-like water,
    Stared in silence

    Till, deformed and pale
In the sunken cavern shadows,
One by one imagined demons
    Scowled upon me.

    Barges passed me by,
With their unknown surly masters
And small cabins, whereon some rude
    Hand had painted

    Trees and castles high.
Cheerly stepped the towing horses,
And the women sung their children
    Into slumber.

    Barges, too, I saw
Drowned in mud, drowned, drowned long ages,
Their grey ribs but seen in summer,
    Their names never:

In whose silted maw
Swarmed great eels, the priests of darkness,
Old as they, who came at midnight
    To destroy me.

Like one blind and lame
Who by some new sense has vision
And strikes deadlier than the strongest
    Went this water.

Many an angler came,
Went his ways; and I would know them,
Some would smile and give me greeting,
    Some kept silence –

Most, one old dragoon
Who had never a morning hallo,
But with stony eye strode onward
    Till the water,

On a silent noon,
That had watched him long, commanded:
Whom he answered, leaping headlong
    To self-murder.

'Fear and fly the spell,'
Thus my Spirit sang beside me;
Then once more I ranged the meadows,
    Yet still brooded,

When the threefold knell
Sounded through the haze of harvest –
Who had found the lame blind water
    Swift and seeing?

The Aftermath

Swift away the century flies,
    Time has yet the wind for wings,
In the past the midnight lies;
    But my morning never springs.

Who goes there? come, ghost or man,
    You were with us, you will know;
Let us commune, there's no ban
    On speech for us if we speak low.

Time has healed the wound, they say,
    Gone's the weeping and the rain;
Yet you and I suspect, the day
    Will never be the same again.

Is it day? I thought there crept
    Some frightened pale rays through the fog,
And where the lank black ash-trees wept
    I thought the birds were just agog.

But no, this fiction died before
    The swirling gloom, as soon as seen;
The thunder's brow, the thunder's roar,
    Darkness that's felt strode swift between.

O euphrasy for ruined eyes!
    I chose, it seemed, a flowering thorn;
The white blooms were but brazen lies,
    The tree I looked upon was torn

In snarling lunacy of pain,
    A brown charred trunk that deadly cowered,
And when I stared across the plain
    Where once the gladdening green hill towered,

It shone a second, then the greed
    Of death had fouled it; dark it stood,
A hump of wilderness untried
    Where the kind Dove would never brood.

Rural Economy (1917)

There was winter in those woods,
    And still it was July:
There were Thule solitudes
    With thousands huddling nigh;
There the fox had left his den,
The scraped holes hid not stoats but men.

To these woods the rumour teemed
    Of peace five miles away;
In sight, hills hovered, houses gleamed
    Where last perhaps we lay
Till the cockerels bawled bright morning and
The hours of life slipped the slack hand.

In sight, life's farms sent forth their gear,
    Here rakes and ploughs lay still;
Yet, save some curious clods, all here
    Was raked and ploughed with a will.
The sower was the ploughman too,
And iron seeds broadcast he threw.

What husbandry could outdo this?
    With flesh and blood he fed
The planted iron that nought amiss
    Grew thick and swift and red,
And in a night though ne'er so cold
Those acres bristled a hundredfold.

Why, even the wood as well as field
    This ruseful farmer knew
Could be reduced to plough and tilled,
    And if he planned, he'd do;
The field and wood, all bone-fed loam,
Shot up a roaring harvest-home.

Water Moment

The silver eel slips through the waving weeds
And in the tunnelled shining stone recedes;
The earnest eye surveys the crystal pond
And guards the cave: the sweet shoals pass beyond.
The watery jewels that these have for eyes,
The tiger streaks of him that hindmost plies,
The red-gold wings that smooth their daring paces,
The sunlight dancing about their airs and graces,
Burn that strange watcher's heart; then the sly brain
Speaks, all the dumb shoal shrieks, and by the stone
The silver death writhes with the chosen one.

The Still Hour

As in the silent darkening room I lay,
While winter's early evening, heavy-paced
As ploughmen from our swarthy soil, groped on
From the cold mill upon the horizon hill
And over paddocks to the neighbouring lodges
And lay as I, tired out with colourless toil,
Inert, the lubber fiend, whose puffing drowse
The moon's dawn scarce would fret, through the low cloud, –
When thus at ebb I lay, my silence flowered
Gently as later bloom into a warm
Harmonious chiming; like a listener I
Was hushed. The spirits of remembrance all
With one consent made music, a flood, a haze,
A vista all to one ripe blushing blended.

That summer veil of sweet sound then awhile
Gave me clear voices, as though from rosy distance
There had been drifting multitude of song,
And then the bells each in his round were heard;
The tower that throned them seen, and even the golden
Chanticleer that frolicked on its top.
From my broad murmuring ode there came fair forth
The cries of playing children on one day,
At one blue dewy hour, by one loved green;
And then the brook was tumbling lit like gems
Down its old sluice, and old boy-heroes stood
To catch its sparkling stonefish – I heard even
The cry that hailed the chestnut tench's downfall
In the next swim, that strange historic victim.
From church and pasture, sweetheart and sworn friend,
From the hill's hopgrounds to the lowest leas
In the rook-routed vale, from the blind boy
Who lived by me to the dwellers in the heath,
From robins building in the gipsy's kettle
Thrown in our hedge, to waterfowl above
The mouldering mill, distinct and happy now
Ten thousand singings from my childhood rang.

And time seemed stealing forward as they sounded,
The syllables of first delights passed;
 Years that ended childhood with their secret sigh
Uttered their joys, still longed-for, still enshrined.
And then what voices? Straight, it seemed, from those,
While a long age was silent as the grave,
The utterance passed to that stern course of chances
That crowded far-off Flanders with ourselves.
I heard the signallers lead the strong battalion
With bold songs flying to the breeze like banners,
The quiet courage once again of Daniells
By some words built up a fort around me,
And while the long guns clattered through the towns
I, rather, heard the clack of market-women,
The hostel's gramophone and gay girls fooling,
And chants in painted churches, and my friend's
Lively review of Flemish contraries.
Or, was not this the green Béthune canal
And these our shouts, our laughs, our awkward plunges,
While summer's day went cloudless to its close?
There shone the Ancre, red-leafed woods above it,
The blue speed of its waters swirled through causeways;
There from his hammock in the apple orchard
Up sprang old Swain and rallied intruding youngsters.
The company now fell in, to the very yard,
And once again marched eager towards the Somme,
And there, a score of voices leapt again
After a hare that left her seat in the corn.
I think I'd know that twinkling field today.

So in swift succession my still hour
Heard Flanders voices, in the line direct
From those of childhood; but at last the host
In such confusion as nigh stopt my breath
With glory and anguish striving, drew far on
And all became a drone, that in decline
From summer's bravery changed to autumn chill,
And as the music vague and piteous grew,
I saw the mist die from its pleasant charm,
Now fierce with early frost its numb shroud lay

Along sad ridges, and as one aloof
I saw the praying rockets mile on mile
Climb all too weak from those entangled there
Climb for the help that could not help them there;
And even these purple vapours died away
And left the surly evening brown as clay
Upon those ridges battered into chaos
Whence one deep moaning, one deep moaning came.

Harvest

So there's my year, the twelvemonth duly told,
Since last I climbed this brow and gloated round
Upon the lands heaped with their wheaten gold,
And now again they spread with wealth imbrowned,
    And thriftless I meanwhile,
What honeycombs have I to take, what sheaves to pile?

I see some shrivelled fruits upon my tree,
And gladly would self-kindness feign them sweet;
The bloom smelled heavenly, can these stragglers be
The fruit of that bright birth? and this wry wheat,
    Can this be from those spires
Which I, or fancy, saw leap to the spring sun's fires?

I peer and count, but anxious is not rich,
My harvest is not come, the weeds run high
Even poison-berries ramping from the ditch
Have stormed the undefended ridges by;
    What Michaelmas is mine!
The fields I thought to serve, for sturdier tillage pine.

But hush – Earth's valleys sweet in leisure lie,
And I among them, wandering up and down,
Will taste their berries, like a bird or fly,
And of their gleanings make both feast and crown;
    The Sun's eye laughing looks,
And Earth accuses none that goes among her stooks.

A Dream

Unriddle this. Last night my dream
Took me along a sullen stream,
A water drifting black and ill,
With idiot swirls, and silent still.
As if it had been Pactolus
And I of gold sands amorous
I went determined on its bank,
Stopped in that breath of dim and dank,
And in my hand (in dream's way) took
A living fish to bait my hook,
A living fish, not gudgeon quite
Nor dace nor roach, a composite;
Then ghoulishly with fingers, yet
With aching mind, I strove to get
The pang of shackling metal through
The mouth of that poor mad perdu,
And (ran the bitter fancy's plot)
To tie his body in a knot.
While thus I groped and grasped and coiled
And he in horror flapped and foiled,
I saw how on the clay around
Young shining fishes leapt and clowned,
And often turned their eyes on me,
Begging their watery liberty,
Most sad and odd. But, thought I, now
I have no time for helping you,
And then at length my bait was hooked,
His shuddering tail grotesquely crooked.
Black was the secret-dimpling stream,
I flounced him to the line's extreme,
And then, his mercy! gladdening me
Who just had been his agony,
Some monstrous mouth beat out his brain,
The line cut wide its graphs of strain.
I knew my prize, and fought my best
With thought and thew – then the fight ceased.
Sobbing I feared the quarry gone,
But no, the dead-weight showed him on,

Slow to the mould I pulled the huge
Half-legend from his subterfuge,
And as he from the water thrust
His head, and cleared its scurf and must,
Two eyes as old as Adam stared
On mine. And now he lay unbared:
My glory! On the bleak bank lay
A carcass effigy in clay,
A trunk of vague and lethal mass
Such as might lie beneath filmed glass,
Where on the pane the buzzing fly
Batters to win the desperate sky.

Intimations of Mortality

– I am only the phrase
    Of an unknown musician;
     By a gentle voice spoken
      I stole forth and met you
  In halcyon days.
Yet, frail as I am, you yourself shall be broken
  Before we are parted; I have but one mission:
     Till death to beset you.

– I am only the glowing
    Of a dead afternoon,
     When you, full of wonder,
      Your hand in your mother's,
  Up great streets were going.
Pale was my flame, and the cold sun fell under
  The blue heights of houses; but I shall gleam on
     In your life past all others.

– I am only the bloom
    Of an apple-tree's roses,
     That stooped to the grass
      Where the robins were nesting
  In an old vessel's womb.
Dead is the tree, and your steps may not pass
  The place where it smiled; but I'll come, till death closes
     My ghostly molesting.

– You phantoms, pursue me,
    Be upon me, amaze me,
     Though nigh all your presence
      With sorrow enchant me,
  With sorrow renew me!
Songless and gleamless, I near no new pleasance,
  In subtle returnings of ecstasy raise me,
     To my winding-sheet haunt me!

Strange Perspective

Happy the herd that in the heat of summer
Wades in the waters where the willows cool them,
From a murmuring midday that singes the meadow;
And naked at noon there naughtiness wantons
From bank bold jumping, and bough down dandling,
Of chimed hour chainless, and churlish duty.
I see the glad set, who am far off sentenced;
Their lily limbs dazzle over long dry pastures,
And, rude though ridges are risen between us,
Miles of mountains morosely upthrusting;
And dim and downward my gaze now droops,
My pool beyond pasture by a strange perspective
Is plain, and plunging its playmates gleam,
Hustling the staid herd into hazardous shadows.

Two Voices

'There's something in the air,' he said
In the large parlour cool and bare,
The plain words in his hearers bred
A tumult, yet in silence there
All waited; wryly gay, he left the phrase,
Ordered the march, and bade us go our ways.

'We're going South, man'; as he spoke
The howitzer with huge ping-bang
Racked the light hut; as thus he broke
The death-news, bright the skylarks sang;
He took his riding-crop and humming went
Among the apple-trees all bloom and scent.

Now far withdraws the roaring night
Which wrecked our flower after the first
Of those two voices; misty light
Shrouds Thiepval Wood and all its worst:
But still 'There's something in the air' I hear,
And still 'We're going South, man,' deadly near.

Preparations for Victory

My soul, dread not the pestilence that hags
The valley; flinch not you, my body young,
At these great shouting smokes and snarling jags
Of fiery iron: the dice may not be flung
As yet that claims you. Manly move among
These ruins, and what you must do, do well;
Look, here are gardens, there mossed boughs are hung
With apples whose bright cheeks none might excel,
And here's a house as yet unshattered by a shell.

'I'll do my best,' the soul makes sad reply,
'And I will mark the yet unmurdered tree,
The tokens of dear homes that court the eye,
And yet I see them not as I would see.
Hovering between, a ghostly enemy
Sickens the light, and poisoned, withered, wan,
The least defiled turns desperate to me.'
The body, poor unpitied Caliban,
Parches and sweats and grunts to win the name of Man.

Hours, days, eternities, like swelling waves
Pass on, and still we drudge in this dark maze,
The bombs and coils and cans by strings of slaves
Are borne to serve the coming day of days;
Grey sleep in slimy cellars scarce allays
With its brief blank the burden. Look, we lose;
The sky is gone, the lightless, drenching haze
Of rainstorms chills the bone; earth, air are foes,
The black fiend leaps brick-red as life's last picture goes.

Zero

O rosy red, O torrent splendour
Staining all the Orient sky,
O celestial work of wonder,
A million mornings in one dye!

What, does the artist of creation
Try some new plethora of flame,
For his eyes' fresh fascination,
Has the old cosmic fire grown tame?

In what subnatural strange awaking
Is this body, which seems mine?
These feet towards that blood-burst making,
These ears which thunder, these hands which twine

On grotesque iron? Icy-clear
The air of a mortal day shocks sense,
My shaking men pant after me here.
The acid vapours hovering dense,

The fury whizzing in dozens down,
The clattering rafters, clods calcined,
The blood in the flints and the trackway brown,
I see I am clothed and in my right mind;

The dawn but hangs behind the goal.
What is that artist's joy to me?
Here limps poor Jock with a gash in the poll,
His red blood now is the red I see.

The swooning white of him, and that red!
These bombs in boxes, the craunch of shells,
The second-hand flitting round; ahead!
It's plain, we were born for this, naught else.

At Senlis Once

O how comely it was and how reviving
When with clay and with death no longer striving
    Down firm roads we came to houses
    With women chattering and green grass thriving.

Now though rains in a cataract descended,
We could glow, with our tribulation ended –
    Count not days, the present only
    Was thought of, how could it ever be expended?

Clad so cleanly, this remnant of poor wretches
Picked up life like the hens in orchard ditches,
    Gazed on the mill-sails, heard the church-bell,
    Found an honest glass all manner of riches.

How they crowded the barn with lusty laughter,
Hailed the pierrots and shook each shadowy rafter,
    Even could ridicule their own sufferings,
    Sang as though nothing but joy came after!

Pillbox

Just see what's happening Worley. – Worley rose
And round the angled doorway thrust his nose,
And Sergeant Hoad went too to snuff the air.
Then war brought down his fist, and missed the pair!
Yet Hoad was scratched by a splinter, the blood came,
And out sprang terrors that he'd striven to tame,
A good man, Hoad, for weeks. I'm blown to bits,
He groans, he screams. Come Bluffer, where's your wits?
Says Worley, Bluffer, you've a blighty, man!
All in the pillbox urged him, here began
His freedom: Think of Eastbourne and your dad.
The poor man lay at length and brief and mad
Flung out his cry of doom; soon ebbed and dumb
He yielded. Worley with a tot of rum
And shouting in his face could not restore him.
The ship of Charon over channel bore him.
All marvelled even on that most deathly day
To see this life so spirited away.

The Welcome

He'd scarcely come from leave and London,
Still was carrying a leather case,
When he surprised Headquarters pillbox
And sat down sweating in the filthy place.

He was a tall, lean, pale-looked creature,
With nerves that seldom ceased to wince,
Past war had long preyed on his nature,
And war had doubled in horror since.

There was a lull, the adjutant even
Came to my hole: 'You cheerful sinner,
If nothing happens till half-past seven,
Come over then, we're going to have dinner.'

Back he went with his fierce red head;
We were sourly canvassing his jauntiness, when
Something happened at Headquarters pillbox.
'Don't go there,' cried one of my men.

The shell had struck right into the doorway,
The smoke lazily floated away;
There were six men in that concrete doorway,
Now a black muckheap blocked the way.

Inside, one who had scarcely shaken
The air of England out of his lungs
Was alive, and sane; it shall be spoken
While any of those who were there have tongues.

The Ancre at Hamel

Where tongues were loud and hearts were light
   I heard the Ancre flow;
Waking oft at the mid of night
   I heard the Ancre flow.
I heard it crying, that sad rill,
   Below the painful ridge,
By the burnt unraftered mill
   And the relic of a bridge.

And could this sighing water seem
   To call me far away,
And its pale word dismiss as dream
   The voices of to-day?
The voices in the bright room chilled
   And that mourned on alone,
The silence of the full moon filled
   With that brook's troubling tone.

The struggling Ancre had no part
   In these new hours of mine,
And yet its stream ran through my heart,
   I heard it grieve and pine,
As if its rainy tortured blood
   Had swirled into my own
When by its battered bank I stood
   And shared its wounded moan.

Country Sale

Under the thin green sky, the twilight day,
The old home lies in public sad array,
Its time being come, the lots ranged out in rows,
And to each lot a ghost. The gathering grows
With every minute, neckcloths and gold pins;
Poverty's purples; red necks, horny skins,
Odd peeping eyes, thin lips and hooking chins.

Then for the skirmish, and the thrusting groups
Bidding for tubs and wire and chicken coops,
While yet the women hang apart and eye
Their friends and foes and reckon who will buy.
The noisy field scarce knows itself, not one
Takes notice of the old man's wavering moan
Who hobbles with his hand still brushing tears
And cries how this belonged here sixty years,
And picks his brother's picture from the mass
Of frames; and still from heap to heap folks pass.

The strife of tongues even tries the auctioneer,
Who, next the dealer smirking to his leer,
A jumped-up jerky cockerel on his box,
Runs all his rigs, cracks all his jokes and mocks;
'Madam, now never weary of well-doing,'
The heavy faces gleam to hear him crowing.
And swift the old home's fading. Here he bawls
The white four-poster, with its proud recalls,
But we on such old-fashioned lumber frown;
'Passing away at a florin,' grins the clown.
Here Baskett's Prayer Book with his black and red
Finds no more smile of welcome than the bed,
Though policeman turn the page with wisdom's looks:
The hen-wives see no sense in such old books.
Here painted trees and well-feigned towers arise,
And ships before the wind, that sixpence buys.

All's sold; then hasty vanmen pile and rope
Their loads, and ponies stumble up the slope
And all are gone, the trampled paddock's bare;
The children round the building run and blare,
Thinking what times these are! not knowing how
The heavy-handed fate has brought them low,
Till quarter loaf be gone too soon today,
And none is due tomorrow. Long, then, play,
And make the lofts re-echo through the eve,
And sweeten so the bitter taking-leave.

So runs the world away. Years hence shall find
The mother weeping to her lonely mind,
In some new place, thin set with makeshift gear,
For the home she had before the fatal year;
And still to this same anguish she'll recur,
Reckoning up her fine old furniture,
The tall clock with his church-bell time of day,
The mirror where so deep the image lay,
The china with its rivets numbered all,
Seeming to have them in her hands – poor soul,
Trembling and crying how these, loved so long,
So beautiful, all went for an old song.

Winter: East Anglia

In a frosty sunset
  So fiery red with cold
The footballers' onset
  Rings out glad and bold;
Then boys from daily tether
  With famous dogs at heel
In starlight meet together
  And to farther hedges steal;
Where the rats are pattering
  In and out the stacks,
Owls with hatred chattering
  Swoop at the terriers' backs
And, frost forgot, the chase grows hot
  Till a rat's a foolish prize,
But the cornered weasel stands his ground,
Shrieks at the dogs and the boys set round,
Shrieks as he knows they stand all round,
  And hard as winter dies.

The Midnight Skaters

The hop-poles stand in cones,
    The icy pond lurks under,
The pole-tops steeple to the thrones
    Of stars, sound gulfs of wonder;
But not the tallest there, 'tis said,
Could fathom to this pond's black bed.

Then is not death at watch
    Within those secret waters?
What wants he but to catch
    Earth's heedless sons and daughters?
With but a crystal parapet
Between, he has his engines set.

Then on, blood shouts, on, on,
    Twirl, wheel and whip above him,
Dance on this ball-floor thin and wan,
    Use him as though you love him;
Court him, elude him, reel and pass,
And let him hate you through the glass.

The Puzzle

The cuckoo with a strong flute,
The orchard with a mild sigh,
Bird and blossom so salute
   The rainbow sky.

The brown herd in the green shade,
The parson in his lawn chair,
Poor and gentry both evade
   The furnace air.

The moon-inveigled mushroom,
The crocus with her frail horn,
Gaze in dumb dread through the gloom
   Of late moist morn.

The dead leaf on the highlands,
The old tramp on the mill drove,
Each whirls on nor understands
   God's freezing love.

Achronos

The trunks of trees which I knew glorious green,
Which I saw felled last year, already show
Rust-red their rounds, the twisting path between
Takes its new way already plain as though
It went this way since years and years ago.
The plough I saw my friend so often guide,
Snapped on the sly snag at the spinney side,
Lies rusting there where brambles overflow;
As gulfed in limbo lake as buried coins,
Which, once both bread and wine, now nothing mean.
The spider dates it not but spins in the heat,
For what's time past? but present time is sweet.
Think, in that churchyard lies fruit of our loins,
– The child who bright as pearl shone into breath
With the Egyptian's first-born shares coeval death.

Warning to Troops

What soldier guessed that where the stream descended
In country dance beneath the colonnade
Of elms which cooled the halted troop, it played
Sly music, barely noted, never ended?
Or who, from war's concerns a moment missed,
At some church door turned white as came to him
One gold note struck by the hidden organist,
One note long-drawn through caverns cool and dim?

O marcher, hear. But when thy route and tramp
Pause by some falling stream, or holy door,
Be the deaf adder; bear not back to camp
That embryo music. Double not thy war.
Shun all such sweet prelusion. March, sing, roar,
Lest perilous silence gnaw thee evermore.

In a Country Churchyard

Earth is a quicksand; yon square tower
    Would still seem bold,
But its bleak flinty strength each hour
    Is losing hold.

Small sound of gasping undertow
    In this green bed!
Who shuts the gate will shut it slow,
    Here sleep the dead.

Here sleep, or slept; here, chance, they sleep,
    Though still this soil
As mad and clammed as shoals acreep
    Around them boil.

The earth slips down to the low brown
    Moss-eaten wall
Each year, and nettles and grasses drown
    Its crumbling crawl.

The dog-rose and ox-daisies on
    Time's tide come twirling,
And bubble and die where Joy is gone –
    Sleep well, my darling.

Seldom the sexton with shrewd grin
    Near thy grave-cloth,
With withered step and mumble thin
    Awakes eve's moth.

Not a farm boy dares here destroy,
    Through red-toothed nettles,
The chiff-chaff's nest, to strew the shells
    Like fallen petals.

The silver-hooded moth upsprings,
    The silver hour,
And wanders on with happy wings
    By the hush tower,

That reels and whirs, and never drops,
    That still is going;
For quicksand not an instant stops
    Its deadly flowing.

And is Joy up and dancing there
    Where deepening blue
Asks a new star? and is that her hair
    There freshed with dew?

Here, O the skull of some small wretch,
    Some slaughtered jot,
Bones white as leaf-strigs or chopped twitch,
    Thus turned fate's plot.

So lies thy skull? This earth, even this
    Like quicksand weaves.
Sleep well, my darling, though I kiss
    Lime or dead leaves.

Sleep in the flux as on the breast,
    In the vortex loll;
In mid simoom, my innocence, rest;
    In lightning's soul

Bower thyself! But, joyous eyes,
    The deeps drag dull –
O morning smile and song, so lies
    Thy tiny skull?

Solutions

The swallow flew like lightning over the green
And through the gate-bars (a hand's breadth between);
He hurled his blackness at that chink and won;
The problem scarcely rose and it was done.

The spider, chance-confronted with starvation,
Took up another airy situation;
His working legs, as it appeared to me,
Had mastered practical geometry.

The old dog dreaming in his frowsy cask
Enjoyed his rest and did not drop his task;
He knew the person of 'no fixed abode,'
And challenged as he shuffled down the road.

These creatures which (Buffon and I agree)
Lag far behind the human faculty
Worked out the question set with satisfaction
And promptly took the necessary action.

By this successful sang-froid I, employed
On 'Who wrote Shakespeare?' justly felt annoyed,
And seeing an evening primrose by the fence
Beheaded it for blooming insolence.

An Infantryman

Painfully writhed the few last weeds upon those houseless uplands,
  Cleft pods had dropt their blackened seeds into the trampled clay,
Wind and rain were running loose, and icy flew the whiplash;
  Masked guns like autumn thunder drummed the outcast year away.

Hidden a hundred yards ahead with winter's blinding passion,
  The mule-beat track appeared half-dead, even war's hot blood
    congealed;
The half-dug trenches brimmed like troughs, the camps lay slushed
    and empty,
  Unless those bitter whistlings proved Death's army in the field.

Over the captured ridge above the hurt battalion waited,
  And hardly had sense left to prove if ghost or living passed
From hole to hole with sunken eyes and slow ironic orders,
  While fiery fountains burst and clanged – and there your lot was
    cast.

Yet I saw your health and youth go brightening to the vortex,
  The ghosts on guard, the storm uncouth were then no match for
    you;
You smiled, you sang, your courage rang, and to this day I hear it,
  Sunny as a may-day dance, along that spectral avenue.

Departure

The beech leaves caught in a moment gust
Run like bowled pennies in the autumn's dust
    And topple; frost like rain
Comes spangling down; through the prismy trees
Phoebus mistakes our horse for his,
    Such glory clothes his mane.

The stream makes his glen music alone
And plays upon shell and pot and stone –
    Our life's after-refrain;
Till in the sky the tower's old song
Reads us the hour, and reads it wrong,
And carter-like comes whistling along
    Our casual Anglian train.

The Match

In a round cavern of glass, in steely water
(None yet so comfortless appalled the day)
A man-eel poised, his lacquer-skin disported
In desert reds and wharfy green; his eyes too
Burned like beads of venom.
Beyond the glass the torturer stood, with thrustings,
Passes, grimaces, toothy grins, warped oeillades.
To this black magic mania's eel retorted
With fierce yet futile muzzle, and lancing darted
In an electric rapine, against the wall
Of glass, or life: those disputants of nothing,
So acidly attracting, lovingly loathing,
Driven by cold radii, goblin lovers, seemed yet
The difficult dumb-show of my generation.

The Zonnebeke Road

Morning, if this late withered light can claim
Some kindred with that merry flame
Which the young day was wont to fling through space!
Agony stares from each grey face,
And yet the day is come; stand down! stand down!
Your hands unclasp from rifles while you can;
The frost has pierced them to the bended bone?
Why see old Stevens there, that iron man,
Melting the ice to shave his grotesque chin!
Go ask him, shall we win?
I never liked this bay, some foolish fear
Caught me the first time that I came in here;
That dugout fallen in awakes, perhaps,
Some formless haunting of some corpse's chaps.
True, and wherever we have held the line,
There were such corners, seeming-saturnine
For no good cause.
                    Now where the Haymarket starts,
There is no place for soldiers with weak hearts;
The minenwerfers have it to the inch.
Look, how the snow-dust whisks along the road,
Piteous and silly; the stones themselves must flinch
In this east wind; the low sky like a load
Hangs over, a dead-weight. But what a pain
Must gnaw where its clay cheek
Crushes the shell-chopped trees that fang the plain –
The ice-bound throat gulps out a gargoyle shriek.
The wretched wire before the village line
Rattles like rusty brambles on dead bine,
And there the daylight oozes into dun;
Black pillars, those are trees where roadways run.
Even Ypres now would warm our souls; fond fool,
Our tour's but one night old, seven more to cool!
O screaming dumbness, O dull clashing death,
Shreds of dead grass and willows, homes and men,
Watch as you will, men clench their chattering teeth
And freeze you back with that one hope, disdain.

Concert Party: Busseboom

The stage was set, the house was packed,
    The famous troop began;
Our laughter thundered, act by act;
    Time light as sunbeams ran.

Dance sprang and spun and neared and fled,
    Jest chirped at gayest pitch,
Rhythm dazzled, action sped
    Most comically rich.

With generals and lame privates both
    Such charms worked wonders, till
The show was over: lagging, loth
    We faced the sunset chill;

And standing on the sandy way,
    With the cracked church peering past,
We heard another matinée,
    We heard the maniac blast

Of barrage south by Saint Eloi,
    And the red lights flaming there
Called madness: Come, my bonny boy,
    And dance to the latest air.

To this new concert, white we stood;
    Cold certainty held our breath;
While men in tunnels below Larch Wood
    Were kicking men to death.

Vlamertinghe: Passing the Château, July 1917

'And all her silken flanks with garlands drest' –
But we are coming to the sacrifice.
Must those have flowers who are not yet gone West?
May those have flowers who live with death and lice?
This must be the floweriest place
That earth allows; the queenly face
Of the proud mansion borrows grace for grace
Spite of those brute guns lowing at the skies.

Bold great daisies' golden lights,
Bubbling roses' pinks and whites –
Such a gay carpet! poppies by the million;
Such damask! such vermilion!
But if you ask me, mate, the choice of colour
Is scarcely right; this red should have been duller.

Gouzeaucourt: the Deceitful Calm

How unpurposed, how inconsequential
Seemed those southern lines when in the pallor
    Of the dying winter
    First we went there!

Grass thin-waving in the wind approached them,
Red roofs in the near view feigned survival,
    Lovely mockers, when we
    There took over.

There war's holiday seemed, nor though at known times
Gusts of flame and jingling steel descended
    On the bare tracks, would you
    Picture death there.

Snow or rime-frost made a solemn silence,
Bluish darkness wrapped in dangerous safety;
    Old hands thought of tidy
    Living-trenches!

There it was, my dears, that I departed,
Scarce a greater traitor ever! There too
    Many of you soon paid for
    That false mildness.

La Quinque Rue

O road in dizzy moonlight bleak and blue,
With forlorn effigies of farms besprawled,
With trees bitterly bare or snapped in two,
Why riddle me thus – attracted and appalled?
For surely now the grounds both left and right
Are tilled, and scarless houses undismayed
Glow in the lustrous mercy of sweet night
And one may hear the flute or fiddle played.
Why lead me then
Through the foul-gorged, the cemeterial fen
To fear's sharp sentries? Why do dreadful rags
Fur these bulged banks, and feebly move to the wind?
That battered drum, say why it clacks and brags?
Another and another! what's behind?
How is it that these flints flame out fire's tongue,
Shrivelling my thought? these collapsed skeletons,
What are they, and these iron hunks among?
Why clink those spades, why glare these startling suns
And topple to the wet and crawling grass,
Where the strange briars in taloned hedges twine?
O road, I know those muttering groups you pass,
I know those moments shrill as shivered glass;
But, I am told, to-night you safely shine
To trim roofs and cropped fields; the error's mine.

'Trench Nomenclature'

Genius named them, as I live! What but genius could compress
In a title what man's humour said to man's supreme distress?
Jacob's Ladder ran reversed, from earth to a fiery pit extending,
With not angels but poor Angles, those for the most part descending.
Thence *Brock's Benefit* commanded endless fireworks by two nations,
Yet some voices there were raised against the rival coruscations.
Picturedrome peeped out upon a dream, not Turner could surpass,
And presently the picture moved, and greyed with corpses and
    morass.
So down south; and if remembrance travel north, she marvels yet
At the sharp Shakespearean names, and with sad mirth her eyes are
    wet.
The Great Wall of China rose, a four-foot breastwork, fronting guns
That, when the word dropped, beat at once its silly ounces with
    brute tons;

Odd *Krab Krawl* on paper looks, and odd the foul-breathed alley
    twisted,
As one feared to twist there too, if *Minnie*, forward quean, insisted.
Where the Yser at *Dead End* floated on its bloody waters
Dead and rotten monstrous fish, note (east) *The Pike and Eel*
    headquarters.
Ah, such names and apparitions! name on name! what's in a name?
From the fabled vase the genie in his shattering horror came.

Another Journey from Béthune to Cuinchy

I see you walking
To a pale petalled sky,
And the green silent water
Is resting there by;
It seems like bold madness
But that 'you' is I.

I long to interpret
That voice of a bell
So silver and simple,
Like a wood-dove-egg shell,
On the bank where you are walking –
It was I heard it well.

At the lock the sky bubbles
Are dancing and dying,
Some the smallest of pearls,
Some moons, and all flying,
Returning and melting –
You watched them, half-crying.

This is Marie-Louise,
You need not have told me –
I remember her eyes
And the Cognac she sold me –
It is you that are sipping it;
Even so she cajoled me.

Her roof and her windows
Were nothing too sound,
And here and there holes
Some forty feet round
(Antiquer than Homer)
Encipher the ground.

Do you jib at my tenses?
Who's who? you or I?
Do you own Béthune
And is that grave eastward sky?
Béthune is miles off now,
'Ware wire and don't die.

The telegraph posts
Have revolted at last,
And old Perpendicular
Leans to the blast,
The rigging hangs ragging
From each plunging mast.

What else would you fancy,
For here it is war?
My thanks, you young upstart,
I've been here before –
I know this Division,
And hate this damned Corps.

'Kingsclere' hath its flowers,
And piano to boot;
The coolest of cellars,
– Your finest salute!
You fraudulent wretch –
You appalling recruit!

O haste, for the darnel
Hangs over the trench,
As yellow as the powder
Which kills with a stench!
Shall you go or I go?
O I'll go – don't mench!

But both of us slither
Between the mossed banks,
And through thirsty chalk
Where the red-hatted cranks
Have fixed a portcullis
With notice-board – thanks!

A mad world, my masters!
Whose masters? my lad,
If you are not I,
It is I who am mad;
Let's report to the company,
Your mess, egad.

Well, now sir (though lime juice
Is nothing to aid),
This young fellow met me,
And kindly essayed
To guide me – but now it seems
I am betrayed.

He says that he is I,
And that I am not he;
But the same omened sky
Led us both, we agree, –
If we cannot commingle,
Pray take him and me.

For where the numb listener
Lies in the dagged weed,
I'll see your word law,
And this youth has agreed
To let me use *his* name –
Take the will for the deed.

And what if the whistle
Of the far-away train
Come moan-like through mist
Over Coldstream Lane,
Come mocking old love
Into waking again?

And the thinkings of life,
Whether those of your blood,
Or the manifold soul
Of field and of flood –
What if they come to you
Bombed in the mud?

Well, now as afore
I should wince so, no doubt,
And still to my star
I should cling, all about,
And muddy one midnight
We all will march out.

– Sir, this man may talk,
But he surely omits
That a shell any moment
May blow us to bits;
On this rock his identity-
Argument splits.

I see him walking
In a golden-green ground,
Where pinafored babies
And skylarks abound,
But that's his own business.
My time for trench round.

Flanders Now

There, where before no master action struck
The grim Fate in the face, and cried 'What now?',
Where gain and commonplace lay in their ruck,
And pulled the beetroots, milked the muddy cow,
Heard the world's rumours, wished themselves good luck,
And slept, and rose, and lived and died somehow, –

A light is striking keen as angels' spears,
Brightness outwelling, cool as roses, there;
From every crossroad majesty appears,
Each cottage gleams like Athens on the air;
Ghosts by broad daylight, answered not by fears
But bliss unwordable, are walking there.

Who thirsts, or aches, or gropes as going blind?
Friend, drink with me at these fair-foliaged wells,
Or on the bruised life lay this unction kind,
Or mark this light that lives in lily-bells,
There rests and always shall the wandering mind,
Those clumsy farms today grow miracles:

Since past each wall and every common mark,
Field path and wooden bridge, there once went by
The flower of manhood, daring the huge dark,
The famished cold, the roaring in the sky;
They died in splendour, these who claimed no spark
Of glory save the light in a friend's eye.

The Watchers

I heard the challenge 'Who goes there?'
Close-kept but mine through midnight air;
I answered and was recognised
And passed, and kindly thus advised:
'There's someone crawlin' through the grass
By the red ruin, or there was,
And them machine guns been a firin'
All the time the chaps was wirin',
So sir if you're goin' out
You'll keep your 'ead well down no doubt.'

When will the stern fine 'Who goes there?'
Meet me again in midnight air?
And the gruff sentry's kindness, when
Will kindness have such power again?
It seems, as now I wake and brood,
And know my hour's decrepitude,
That on some dewy parapet
The sentry's spirit gazes yet,
Who will not speak with altered tone
When I at last am seen and known.

The Author's Last Words to His Students

Forgive what I, adventuring highest themes,
   Have spoiled and darkened, and the awkward hand
That longed to point the moral of man's dreams
   But shut the wicket-gates of fairyland:
      So by too harsh intrusion
      Left colourless confusion.

For even the glories that I most revered,
   Seen through my gloomed perspective in strange mood,
Were not what to our British seers appeared;
   I spoke of peace, I made a solitude,
      Herding with deathless graces
      My hobbling commonplaces.

Forgive that eyeless lethargy which chilled
   Your ardours and I fear dimmed much fine gold –
What your bright passion, leaping ages, thrilled
   To find and claim, and yet I dared withhold;
      These and all chance offences
      Against your finer senses.

And I will ever pray for your souls' health,
   Remembering how, deep-burdened, eager-eyed,
You loved imagination's commonwealth,
   Following with smiling wonder that frail guide
      Who hears beyond the ocean
      The voice of your devotion.

Familiarity

Dance not your spectral dance at me;
I know you well!
Along this lane there lives no tree
But I can tell.
I know each fall and rise and twist;
You – why, a wildflower in the mist,
The moon, the mist.

Sound not that long alarm, grey tower,
I know you well;
This is your habit at this hour,
You and your bell!
If once, I heard a hundred times
Through evening's ambuscade your chimes –
Dark tower, your chimes.

Enforce not that no-meaning so,
Familiar stream;
Whether you tune it high or low,
I know your theme;
A proud-fed but a puny rill,
A meadow brook, poured quick and shrill –
Alone and shrill.

Sprawl not so monster-like, blind mist;
I know not 'seems';
I am too old a realist
To take sea-dreams
From you, or think a great white Whale
Floats through our hawthorn-scented vale –
This foam-cold vale.

A Sunrise in March

While on my cheek the sour and savage wind
Confuses soul with sense, while unamazed
I view the siege of pale-starred horror raised
By dawn whose waves charge stern and crimson-lined,
In cold blue tufts of battle-smoke afar,
And sable crouching thickets by my way –
While I thus droop, the living land grows gay
With starry welcomes to the conquering star!
From every look-out whence they watch him win
(That angry Cromwell!) high on thorn and bine
The selfless wildbirds hail their holy light:
With changes free as flute or violin,
To naked fields they peal as proud and fine
As though they had not dreamed of death all night.

The Kiln

Beside the creek where seldom oar or sail
Adventures, and the gulls whistling like men
Patrol the pasture of the falling tide,
Like Timon's mansion stands the silent kiln.
Half citadel, half temple, strong it stands
With layered stones built into cavernous curves,
The fire-vault now as cool as leaves and stones
And dews can be. Here came my flitting thought,
The only visitor of a sunny day,
Except the half-mad wasp that fights with all,
The leaping cricket in his apple-green,
And emerald beetle with his golden helmet;
While the south wind woke all the colony
Of sorrels and sparse daisies, berried ivies
And thorns bowed down with sloes, and brambles red
Offering a feast that no child came to take.

In these unwanted derelicts of man
Nature has touched the picture with a smile
Of more than usual mystery; the far heights
With thunderous forest marshalled are her toil,
But this her toy, her petty larceny
That pleased her, lurking like a gipsy girl.
My thought came here with artfulness like hers
To spy on her, and, though she fled, pursued
To where on eastern islands, in the cells
Of once grave seers, her iris woos the wind.

The Correlation

Again that yellow dusk or light along
The winter hills: again the trees' black claws
Waiting and working by the bridge of space:
Again the tower, among tombs a huge tomb;
White scattered birds, a black horse in the meads,
And the eel-track of the brown stream fringing by.

Would understanding win herself my vote,
Now, having known this crisis thirty years,
She should decide me why it overwhelms
My chart of time and history; should declare
What in the spirit of a man long schooled
To human concept and devotion dear,
Upraised by sure example, undefiled
By misery and defeat, still in the sun –
What stirs in him, and finds its brother-self,
From that late sky. Again that sky, that tower
These effigies and wizardries of chance,
Those soundless vollies of pale and distant birds
Have taken him, and from his whirring toils
Made him as far away, as unconcerned,
As consonant with the Power as its bare trees.

The Deeper Friendship

Were all eyes changed, were even poetry cold,
Were those long systems of hope that I tried to deploy
Skeletons, still I should keep one final hold,
Since clearer and clearer returns my first-found joy.

I would go, once more, through the sunless autumn in trouble;
Thin and cold rain dripping down through branches black,
Streams hoarse-hurrying and pools spreading over the stubble,
And the waggoner leaving the hovel under his sack

Would guide me along by the gate and deserted siding,
The inn with the tattered arbour, the choking weir;
And yet, security there would need small guiding.
I know one hearth, one love that shine beyond fear.

There, though the sharpest storm and flood were abroad,
And the last husk and leaf were stripped from the tree,
I would sue for peace where the rats and mice have gnawed,
And well content that Nature should bury me.

The Blind Lead the Blind

Dim stars like snowflakes are fluttering in heaven,
Down the cloud-mountains by wind-torrents riven;
There are still chances, but one more than all
Slowly burns out on the sea's dark wall –
    The best ever given.

One, the divinest, goes down to the dark,
In a red sullen vanishing, a poor stifled spark.
You, who have reason, were staring at this
As though by your gaze it would clear the abyss –
    It was once your sea-mark.

Hear on the shore too the sighed monotones
Of waves that in weakness slip past the purled stones;
The seethe of blown sand round the dry fractured hull,
Salt-reeds and tusked fence; hear the struck gull
    With death in his bones.

Slow comes the net in, that's filled with frustration;
Night ends the day of thwart discreation;
I would be your miracle-worker, sad friend,
Bid a music for you and a new star ascend, –
    But I know isolation.

Report on Experience

I have been young, and now am not too old;
And I have seen the righteous forsaken,
His health, his honour and his quality taken.
      This is not what we were formerly told.

I have seen a green country, useful to the race,
Knocked silly with guns and mines, its villages vanished,
Even the last rat and the last kestrel banished –
      God bless us all, this was peculiar grace.

I knew Seraphina; Nature gave her hue,
Glance, sympathy, note, like one from Eden.
I saw her smile warp, heard her lyric deaden;
      She turned to harlotry; – this I took to be new.

Say what you will, our God sees how they run.
These disillusions are His curious proving
That He loves humanity and will go on loving;
      Over there are faith, life, virtue in the sun.

A Connoisseur

Presume not that grey idol with the scythe
And hourglass of the stern perpetual sands
To be a mere insensate mill of hours,
Unawed by battles, unbeguiled with flowers;
Think, this old Merlin may be vexed or blithe,
And for the future stretches hungry hands.

No last year's bride discovers more caprice
Than this bald magpie smuggling up his wit,
And in his crumbling belfry, where the cost
Of high-born death in plundered ruin's lost,
Nodding his glory to each glittering piece
Of glass or jewel that his fancy hit.

Close in the shop of some lean artisan,
Who carves a snuff-box for Squire Harkaway,
Time stoops, and stares, and knows his destined prize:
Croesus shall hunt this modest merchandise
When frieze and pillar of a master's plan
Are crushed in waggon-tracks to bind the clay.

There stalled theology makes angels weep
In twenty volumes blazoned red and gold,
And there a broadside's bawled about the street;
Time fetched his halfpence out and bought a sheet.
The twenty volumes slumber in a heap,
The ballad among heirlooms lives enrolled.

Lordly oration thronged the sculptured roof,
And pamphleteered in plaudits through the town;
The charlatan proclaimed his draughts and pills,
And tossed the crowd his woodcuts and his bills;
From rhetoric's remains Time flies aloof,
And hears the quack still pattering to the clown.

Voluptuous canvas! Venus in May-bloom,
Sunshine of vital gold, faun-twinkling groves,
Harmonious limbs and volant veils, go mourn;
For you will lie with fire, while Time has borne
The blue-daubed frigate from the servants' room
To swell the mad collection of his loves.

Values

Till darkness lays a hand on these grey eyes
And out of man my ghost is sent alone,
It is my chance to know that force and size
Are nothing but by answered undertone.
No beauty even of absolute perfection
Dominates here – the glance, the pause, the guess
Must be my amulets of resurrection;
Raindrops may murder, lightning may caress.

There I was tortured, but I cannot grieve;
There crowned and palaced – visibles deceive.
That storm of belfried cities in my mind
Leaves me my vespers cool and eglantined.
From love's wide-flowering mountain-side I chose
This sprig of green, in which an angel shows.

Into the Salient

Sallows like heads in Polynesia,
With few and blood-stuck hairs,
Mud-layered cobble-stones,
Soldiers in smoky sheds, blackening uniforms and walls with their
    cookery;
Shell-holes in roofs, in roads,
Even in advertisements
Of bicycles and beer;
The Middle Ages gone to sleep, and woken up to this, –
A salvo, four flat slamming explosions.
When you come out the wrong side of the ruin, you are facing Hill
    Sixty,
Hill Sixty is facing you.
You have been planted on the rim of a volcano,
Which will bring forth its fruit – at any second.
Better to be shielded from these facts;
There is a cellar, or was just now.
If the wreck isn't knocked in on us all,
We may emerge past the two Belgian policemen,
The owners' representatives,
Standing in their capes on the steps of the hollow estaminet
Open at all hours to all the winds
At the Poperinghe end of Ypres.
O if we do, if time will pass in time,
We will march
With rifles butt-upwards, in our teeth, any way you like,
Into seven days of country where you come out any door.

Premature Rejoicing

What's that over there?
                    Thiepval Wood.
Take a steady look at it; it'll do you good.
Here, these glasses will help you. See any flowers?
There sleeps Titania (correct – the Wood is ours);
There sleeps Titania in a deep dugout,
Waking, she wonders what all the din's about,
And smiles through her tears, and looks ahead ten years,
And sees her Wood again, and her usual Grenadiers,
        All in green,
        Music in the moon;
    The burnt rubbish you've just seen
    Won't beat the Fairy Queen;
        All the same, it's a shade too soon
        For you to scribble rhymes
        In your army book
        About those times;
        Take another look;
That's where the difficulty is, over there.

To Joy

        Is not this enough for moan
        To see this babe all motherless –
        A babe beloved – thrust out alone
            Upon death's wilderness?
        Our tears fall, fall, fall – I would weep
        My blood away to make her warm,
        Who never went on earth one step,
            Nor heard the breath of the storm.
        How shall you go, my little child,
        Alone on that most wintry wild?

A Japanese Evening

Round us the pines are darkness
That with a wild melodious piping rings
While in the ditches
Slow as toads in English gardens
The little landcrabs move.
We re-discover our path,
And, coming to the cottage, are greeted
With hierophantic usherings and oracles,
And a grin behind the screen, I imagine.
We guess full fathom five, and take up the chopsticks.
The metal-blue cucumber slices,
Rice, string beans,
And green tea over,
The housekeeper looking kindly amazement
At the master of the house
Soon makes all shipshape.
After all, they possess an American clock,
A very fine, a high-collar clock.
She sits on the mat, awaiting the next oddity.

Lanterns moon the outer darkness,
And merrily in come floating
(So gently they foot the honourable straw)
Three young girls, who sit them down.
A conference;
Almost the Versailles of the Far East:
The master, beaming,
His white hair in the lamplight seeming brighter with his pleasure,
Asks me what I call O tsuki sama.
Moon.
Mooon.
Moon.
He has got it; right first time,
But not the next.

Moooni.
(The housekeeper cannot suppress her giggles,
Okashii, she says, and so it is.)

We now pass naturally to the
Electric Light.
But he will not have that,
There are no things like that in heaven and earth
In his philology.
I repeat – what I said;
He repeats – what he said.
We close at Erecturiku Rightu.
We fasten also on:
The cat, who becomes catsu,
The dog, who proceeds doggi,
(And I suspect has rabies beginning);
Himself, O-Ji-San, Orudu Genturuman,
And all sorts of enigmas.

The girls are quicker, more nimble-throated,
And will reproduce exactly the word, but he lays the law down;
Having re-orientated Fan,
Which they pronounced Fan,
Into Weino,
He instructs them how it ought to be pronounced,
Obediently young Japan reiterates his decision,
Not without an ocular hint to the stranger
That they have concealed the other rendering in their minds …
I hear their voices tinkling, lessening
Over the firefly grass,
Along the seething sand below the pines,
At the end of the entertainment.

Under a Thousand Words

'A thousand words on Courage.' – This request
Dropped on me like a bomb on a sandbag shelter,
And after much vague mental repetition
Ranging from La Boisselle to Lord Macaulay,
And metaphysical cross-examination
On memories of conspicuous gallant conduct,
I gave it up.
                    That afternoon our boat
Touched on a mud-flat, which we chose to cross,
And as we waddled through it, a three-inch crab
Disputed progress; one of his arms was gone;
The other he held ready like a boxer,
And backed and sidled to our every movement,
His one arm ready; and to command full view
Of the two monsters who had crossed the frontier,
He strained his body backward, and stood tilted,
Parrying every stroke we acted at him,
Eyeing us, holding the line.
                              'But you call this instinct.'

The Sunlit Vale

I saw the sunlit vale, and the pastoral fairy-tale;
The sweet and bitter scent of the may drifted by;
And never have I seen such a bright bewildering green,
     But it looked like a lie,
     Like a kindly meant lie.

When gods are in dispute, one a Sidney, one a brute,
It would seem that human sense might not know, might not spy;
But though nature smile and feign where foul play has stabbed and
    slain,
     There's a witness, an eye,
     Nor will charms blind that eye.

Nymph of the upland song and the sparkling leafage young,
For your merciful desire with these charms to beguile,
For ever be adored; muses yield you rich reward;
     But you fail, though you smile –
     That other does not smile.

Incident in Hyde Park, 1803

The impulses of April, the rain-gems, the rose-cloud,
The frilling of flowers in the westering love-wind!
And here through the Park come gentlemen riding,
And there through the Park come gentlemen riding,
And behind the glossy horses Newfoundland dogs follow.
Says one dog to the other, 'This park, sir, is mine, sir.'
The reply is not wanting; hoarse clashing and mouthing
Arouses the masters.
Then Colonel Montgomery, of the Life Guards, dismounts.
'Whose dog is this?' The reply is not wanting,
From Captain Macnamara, Royal Navy: 'My dog.'
'Then call your dog off, or by God he'll go sprawling.'
'If my dog goes sprawling, you must knock me down after.'
'Your name?' 'Macnamara, and yours is – ' 'Montgomery.'
'And why, sir, not call your dog off?' 'Sir, I chose
Not to do so, no man has dictated to me yet,

And you, I propose, will not change that.' 'This place,
For adjusting disputes, is not proper' – and the Colonel,
Back to the saddle, continues, 'If your dog
Fights my dog, I warn you, I knock your dog down.
For the rest, you are welcome to know where to find me,
Colonel Montgomery; and you will of course
Respond with the due information.' 'Be sure of it.'
Now comes the evening, green-twinkling, clear-echoing,
And out to Chalk-farm the Colonel, the Captain,
Each with his group of believers, have driven.
    Primrose Hill on an April evening
      Even now in a fevered London
   Sings a vesper sweet; but these
     Will try another music. Hark!
These are the pistols; let us test them; quite perfect.
Montgomery, Macnamara six paces, two faces;
Montgomery, Macnamara – both speaking together
In nitre and lead, the style is incisive,
Montgomery fallen, Macnamara half-falling,
The surgeon exploring the work of the evening –
And the Newfoundland dogs stretched at home in the firelight.

The coroner's inquest; the view of one body;
And then, pale, supported, appears at Old Bailey
James Macnamara, to whom this arraignment:
    You stand charged
    That you
    With force and arms
    Did assault Robert Montgomery,
    With a certain pistol

    Of the value of ten shillings,
    Loaded with powder and a leaden bullet,
    Which the gunpowder, feloniously exploded,
    Drove into the body of Robert Montgomery,
    And gave
    One mortal wound;
    Thus you did kill and slay
    The said Robert Montgomery.

O heavy imputation! O dead that yet speaks!
O evening transparency, burst to red thunder!

Speak, Macnamara. He, tremulous as a windflower,
Exactly imparts what had slaughtered the Colonel,
'Insignificant the origin of the fact now before you;
Defending our dogs, we grew warm; that was nature;
That heat of itself had not led to disaster.
From defence to defiance was the leap that destroyed.
At once he would have at my deity, Honour –
"If you are offended you know where to find me."
On one side, I saw the wide mouths of Contempt,
Mouth to mouth working, a thousand vile gunmouths;
On the other my Honour; Gentlemen of the Jury,
I am a Captain in the British Navy.'

Then said Lord Hood: 'For Captain Macnamara,
He is a gentleman and so says the Navy.'
Then said Lord Nelson: 'I have known Macnamara
Nine years, a gentleman, beloved in the Navy,
Not to be affronted by any man, true,
Yet as I stand here before God and my country,

Macnamara has never offended, and would not,
Man, woman, child.' Then a spring-tide of admirals,
Almost Neptune in person, proclaim Macnamara
Mild, amiable, cautious, as any in the Navy;
And Mr. Garrow rises, to state that if need be,
To assert the even temper and peace of his client,
He would call half the Captains in the British Navy.

Now we are shut from the duel that Honour
Must fight with the Law; no eye can perceive
The fields wherein hundreds of shadowy combats
Must decide between a ghost and a living idolon –
A ghost with his army of the terrors of bloodshed,
A half-ghost with the grand fleet of names that like sunrise
Have dazzled the race with their march on the ocean.

Twenty minutes. How say you?
                              Not guilty.

Then from his chair with his surgeon the Captain
Walks home to his dog, his friends' acclamations
Supplying some colour to the pale looks he had,
Less pale than Montgomery's; and Honour rides on.

Winter Stars

Fierce in flaming millions, ready to strike they stood,
The stars of unknown will, above our field and wood;
You who have seen the midnight preparing a dawn of war
May raise imagination to see them ready to roar
Their sparkling death-way down; and while they waited the order
Some came flying from nowhere, and launched what looked like
    murder,
Rushing beyond our border, and detonating too far
For us to hear. No need to hear. Watching each angry star
I thought our thicket lifted its stack of bayonets
Stiffly against the overthrow of Nature's parapets;
And marching amain from the highlands came our stream to see
    this through;
Deep and hoarse and gathering force, it swore to die or do;
Under the intelligence of strange foes, it sang to itself and chance,
Answering all that wildfire with the gleam of its foaming advance.

The Kiss

I am for the woods against the world,
    But are the woods for me?
I have sought them sadly anew, fearing
    My fate's mutability,
Or that which action and process make
    Of former sympathy.

Strange that those should arrive strangers
    Who were once entirely at home.
Colonnade, sunny wall and warren,
    Islet, osier, foam,
Buds and leaves and selves seemed
    Safe to the day of doom.

By-roads following, and this way wondering,
    I spy men abroad
In orchards, knarred and woody men
    Whose touch is bough and bud;
Co-arboreal sons of landscape.
    Then in windstript wood

Is the cracking of stems; and under the thorn
    With a kobold's closeness lurks
The wanderer with his knife and rods,
    That like a bald rook works;
His woman-rook about the thicket
    Prowls at the hazel-forks.

Sheep lying out by the swollen river
    Let the flood roll down
Without so much as a glance; they know it;
    The hurling seas of brown
Cannot persuade the ferrying moorhen
    Her one willow will drown.

This way wondering, I renew
    Some sense of common right;
And through my armour of imposition
    Win the Spring's keen light,
Till for the woods against the world
    I kiss the aconite.

The Recovery

From the dark mood's control
  I free my limbs; there's light still in the West.
The most virtuous, chaste, melodious soul
  Never was better blest.

Here medicine for the mind
  Lies in a gilded shade; this feather stirs
And my faith lives; the touch of this tree's rind, –
  And temperate sense recurs.

No longer the loud pursuit
  Of self-made clamour dulls the ear; here dwell
Twilight societies, twig, fungus, root,
  Soundless, and speaking well.

Beneath the accustomed dome
  Of this chance-planted, many-centuried tree
The snake-marked earthly multitudes are come
  To breathe their hour like me.

The leaf comes curling down,
  Another and another, gleam on gleam;
Above, celestial leafage glistens on,
  Borne by time's blue stream.

The meadow-stream will serve
  For my refreshment; that high glory yields
Imaginings that slay; the safe paths curve
  Through unexalted fields

Like these, where now no more
  My early angels walk and call and fly,
But the mouse stays his nibbling, to explore
  My eye with his bright eye.

The Memorial, 1914–1918

Against this lantern, shrill, alone
The wind springs out of the plain.
Such winds as this must fly and moan
Round the summit of every stone
On every hill; and yet a strain
Beyond the measure elsewhere known
Seems here.
              Who cries? who mingles with the gale?
Whose touch, so anxious and so weak, invents
A coldness in the coldness? in this veil
Of whirling mist what hue of clay consents?
Can atoms intercede?

And are those shafted bold constructions there,
Mines more than golden, wheels that outrace need,
Crowded corons, victorious chimneys – are
Those touched with question too? pale with the dream
Of those who in this aether-stream
Are urging yet their painful, wounded theme?

Day flutters as a curtain, stirred
By a hidden hand; the eye grows blurred.
Those towers, uncrystalled, fade.
The wind from the north and east and south
Comes with its starved white mouth
And at this crowning trophy cannot rest –
No, speaks as something past plain words distressed.

Be still, if these your voices are; this monolith
For you and your high sleep was made.
Some have had less.
No gratitude in deathlessness?
No comprehension of the tribute paid?

You would speak still? Who with?

November 1, 1931

We talked of ghosts; and I was still alive;
And I that very day was thirty-five;
Alone once more, I stared about my room
And wished some ghost would be a friend and come;
I cared not of what shape or semblance; terror
Was nothing in comparison with error;
I wished some ghost would come, to talk of fate,
And tell me why I drove my pen so late,
And help with observations on my knack
Of being always on the bivouac,
Here and elsewhere, for ever changing ground,
Finding and straightway losing what I found,
Baffled in time, fumbling each sequent date,
Mistaking Magdalen for the Menin Gate.
This much I saw without transmortal talk,
That war had quite changed my sublunar walk —
Forgive me, dear, honoured and saintly friends;
Ingratitude suspect not; this transcends.
Forgive, O sweet red-smiling love, forgive,
If this is life, for your delight I live;
How every lamp, how every pavement flames
Your beauty at me, and your faith acclaims!
But from my silences your kindness grew,
And I surrendered for the time to you,
And still I hold you glorious and my own,
I'd take your hands, your lips; but I'm alone.
So I was forced elsewhere, and would accost
For colloquy and guidance some kind ghost.
As one that with a serious trust was sent
Afar, and bandits seized him while he went,
And long delayed, so I; I yearned to catch
What I should know before my grave dispatch
Was to be laid before that General
Who in a new Time cries 'backs to the wall'.
No ghost was granted me; and I must face
Uncoached the masters of that Time and Space,
And there with downcast murmurings set out
What my gross late appearance was about.

The Surprise

Shot from the zenith of desire
    Some faultless beams found where I lay,
Not much expecting such white fire
    Across a slow close working-day.

What great song then sang the brook,
    The fallen pillar's grace how new;
The vast white oaks like cowslips shook –
    And I was winged, and flew to you.

The Cottage at Chigasaki

That well you drew from is the coldest drink
In all the country Fuji looks upon;
And me, I never come to it but I think
The poet lived here once who one hot noon
Came dry and eager, and with wonder saw
The morning glory about the bucket twined,
Then with a holy heart went out to draw
His gallon where he might; the poem's signed
By him and Nature. We need not retire,
But freely dip, and wash away the salt
And sand we've carried from the sea's blue fire;
Discuss a melon; and without great fault,
Though comfort is not poetry's best friend,
We'll write a poem too, and sleep at the end.

Lark Descending

A singing firework; the sun's darling;
    Hark how creation pleads!
Then silence: see, a small grey bird
    That runs among the weeds.

The Branch Line

Professing loud energy, out of the junction departed
The branch-line engine. The small train rounded the bend
Watched by us pilgrims of summer, and most by me, –
Who had known this picture since first my travelling started,
And knew it as sadly pleasant, the usual end
Of singing returns to beloved simplicity.

The small train went from view behind the plantation,
Monotonous, – but there's a grace in monotony!
I felt its journey, I watched in imagination
Its brown smoke spun with sunshine wandering free
Past the great weir with its round flood-mirror beneath,
And where the magpie rises from orchard shadows,
And among the oasts, and like a rosy wreath
Mimicking children's flower-play in the meadows.

The thing so easy, so daily, of so small stature
Gave me another picture: of war's warped face
Where still the sun and the leaf and the lark praised nature,
But no little engine bustled from place to place;
Then summer succeeded summer, yet only ghosts
Or tomorrow's ghosts could venture hand or foot
In the track between the terrible telegraph-posts, –
The end of all things lying between the hut
Which lurked this side, and the shattered local train
That.
        So easy it was; and should that come again –.

The Lost Battalion

'To dream again.' That chance. There were no fences,
No failures, no impossibles, no tenses.
Here's the huge sulky ship, the captain's room,
The swilling decks like hillsides, the iron boom
Of ocean's pugilism, black faces, low
Corner-cabals – 'Where are we bound? d'ye know?'
And now, long months being drummed into our lives,
The bells ring back and fro, the boat arrives –
We've seen this place, does no one know its *name*?
Name missing. But we'll get there all the same.
It's all the same. I thought the war was done.
We'll have to hurry, the Battalion's gone.
How on again? Only an Armistice.
I thought my nerves weren't quite so bad as this.
That white house hangs on strangely, turn sharp right,
And the instant war spreads grey and mute in sight.
I feel my old gear on my back, and know
My general job in this forthcoming show;
But what's the catch, the difference? Someone speak!
Name wanted, or I shan't get there this week.

At Rugmer

Among sequestered farms and where brown orchards
Weave in the thin and coiling wind, and where
The pale cold river ripples still as moorhens
Work their restless crossing,
Among such places, when October warnings
Sound from each kex and thorn and shifting leaf,
We well might wander, and renew some stories
Of a dim time when we were kex and thorn,
Sere leaf, ready to hear a hissing wind
Whip down and wipe us out; our season seemed
At any second closing.
So, we were wrong. But we have lived this landscape,
And have an understanding with these shades.

An Ominous Victorian

I am the *Poems of* the late *Eliza Cook*,
For sixty odd years I have occupied this nook;
I remember myself as a bright young book
    On a bookseller's ormolu table.

Just beside me I had quite a nice friend,
Mrs. Hemans's Works, and at the far end
Was one called *It's Never Too Late to Mend*,
    And a print of the Tower of Babel.

We were a pretty pair, *Mrs. H.* and I,
My crimson velvet was the best you could buy;
She wore green – and a love of a tie, –
    I suppose it would now look tawdry.

One fine morning she was taken, as I heard,
For a prize to a Miss Georgiana Bird.
Then my turn came – I'd to carry the word
    Of 'Podgers, with love to Audrey.'

Some little time I was much in request,
Either she read me or hugged me to her breast,
And several sorts of ferns were pressed
    Between my red-ruled pages.

O if only I could warn some of you young books,
Who are taken in like me by loving looks,
–There was no name then like *Eliza Cook's*;
    It's preparedness that assuages.

Then, one night (I can almost see it still)
A letter came; she put down her quill,
And read, and stormed, 'I should like to kill
    That two-faced miscreant Podgers';

And she flung me under the settee, where
I lay in want of light and air,
Enduring the supercilious stare
    Of the *Works of Samuel Rogers*

That always stood on the bracket – well,
There's not much really left to tell,
I was rescued by the housemaid Nell
    Who hadn't no time for reading,

But on the whatnot made me do
For a lamp (of the horridest butcher-blue)
To stand on; and she shrouded me, too,
    In a mat of her mother's beading.

And here I am, and yet I suppose
I'd better not grumble, as this world goes,
For I see I'm outstaying rows and rows
    Of the newest immortal fiction;

And *Rogers* has vanished – I don't know where –
With his *Pleasures of Memory* – and I don't care;
I presume he's propping the leg of a chair
    With his sniffy elegant diction.

Late Light

Come to me where the swelling wind assails the wood with a
     sea-like roar,
While the yellow west is still afire; come borne by the wind up
     the hillside track;
  There is quiet yet, and brightness more
  Than day's clear fountains to noon rayed back
    If you will come;

  If you will come, and against this fall
  Of leaves and light and what seemed time,
  Now changed to haste, against them all
  Glow, calm and young; O help me climb
  Above the entangling phantoms harrying
  Shaken ripeness, unsighted prime;
  Come unwithering and unvarying –
  Tell claw-handed Decline to scrawl
  A million menaces on the wall
  For whom it will; while safe we two
  Move where no knife-gust ever blew,
  And no boughs crack, and no bells toll,
  Through the tempest's ominous interval,
    Penitential low recall.

Writing a Sketch of a Forgotten Poet

Here this great summer day,
    While the fields are wild
With flowers you name, I stay,
    And have learnedly compiled

From shaky books, too few,
    Dry registers,
Something of the living you;
    And have gleaned your verse.

You might have laughed to see,
    With this rich sun,
One pent in a library
    Who else might run

Free in the flashing sweet
    Life-lavishing air.
Or, lover of books, you'd greet
    Such constancy and care.

You might have laughed to hear
    Your stanzas read –
If it were not so clear
    The dead are dead.

What gulfs between us lie!
    I had thought them crossed,
Dreaming to gratify
    Your unimpatient ghost.

In My Time

Touched with a certain silver light
In each man's retrospection,
There are important hours; some others
Seem to grow kingfisher's feathers,
Or glow like sunflowers; my affection
In the first kind finds more delight.

I would not challenge you to discover
Finally why you dwell
In this ward or that of your experience.
Men may vary without variance.
Each vase knows the note, the bell,
Which thrills it like a lover.

When I am silent, when a distance
Dims my response, forgive;
Accept that when the past has beckoned,
There is no help; all else comes second;
Agree, the way to live
Is not to dissect existence.

All the more waive common reason
If the passion when revealed
Seem of poor blood; if the silver hour
Be nothing but an uncouth, shot-torn tower,
And a column crossing a field,
Bowed men, to a dead horizon.

Minority Report

That you have given us others endless means
To modify the dreariness of living,
Machines which even change men to machines;
That you have been most honourable in giving;
That thanks to you we roar through space at speed
Past dreams of wisest science not long since,
And listen in to news we hardly need,
And rumours that might make Horatius wince,
Of modes of sudden death devised by you,
And promising protection against those –
All this and more I know, and what is due
Of praise would offer, couched more fitly in prose.
But such incompetence and such caprice
Clog human nature that, for all your kindness,
Some shun loud-speakers as uncertain peace,
And fear flood-lighting is a form of blindness;
The televisonary world to come,
The petrol-driven world already made,
Appear not to afford these types a crumb
Of comfort. You will win; be not dismayed.
Let those pursue their fantasy, and press
For obsolete illusion, let them seek
Mere moonlight in the last green loneliness;
Your van will be arriving there next week.

'Can You Remember?'

Yes, I still remember
    The whole thing in a way;
Edge and exactitude
    Depend on the day.

Of all that prodigious scene
    There seems scanty loss,
Though mists mainly float and screen
    Canal, spire and fosse;

Though commonly I fail to name
    That once obvious Hill,
And where we went and whence we came
    To be killed, or kill.

Those mists are spiritual
    And luminous-obscure,
Evolved of countless circumstance
    Of which I am sure;

Of which, at the instance
    Of sound, smell, change and stir,
New-old shapes for ever
    Intensely recur.

And some are sparkling, laughing, singing,
    Young, heroic, mild;
And some incurable, twisted,
    Shrieking, dumb, defiled.

On a Picture by Dürer

Sonnenuntergang

Where found you, Dürer, that strange group of trees,
That seared, shamed, mutilated group still standing
To tell us *This is War*: where found you these?
I did not guess, when last I saw shells landing
Smash on the track beside, how old they were.
They had been good tall pines, I saw, but not
Of such great bole as argued they stood there
When your antiquity might pass the spot.

A thousand of us who as yet survive
From what was modern war the other day
Could recognise them, killed in the great Drive
Which strewed so many bones in glory's way.
But, you, your date was wrong. From which of your towers
Saw you that night across the centuries,
Under that cloud with baleful eye slits, ours –
Our sign, our shape, our dumb but eloquent trees?

Cricket, I Confess

'Sir, I cannot profess to understand
One thing in England' – and Sakabé scanned
My face to be sure there was no offence astir, –
'It is Cricket, I confess. In the English character
That's the chief puzzle I have. "My horn is dry,"
If you don't understand it, no more do I.'
Far out in the valley the sun was gilding green
Those meadows which in England most are seen,
Where churchyard, church, inn, forge and loft stand round
With cottages, and through the ages bound
The duckpond, and the stocks, and cricket-ground.
And I fell silent, while kind memories played
Bat and ball in the sunny past, not much dismayed
Why these things were, and why I liked them so.
O my Relf and Jessop and Hutchings long ago.

To W.O. and His Kind

If even you, so able and so keen,
And master of the business you reported
Seem now almost as though you had never been,
And in your simple purpose nearly thwarted,
What hope is there? What harvest from those hours
Deliberately, and in the name of truth,
Endured by you? Your witness moves no Powers,
And younger youth resents your sentient youth.

You would have stayed me with some parable,
The grain of mustard seed, the boy that thrust
His arm into the leaking dyke to quell
The North Sea's onrush. Would you were not dust.
With you I might invent, and make men try,
Some kindly shelter from this frantic sky.

In May 1916: Near Richebourg St Vaast

The green brook played, talked unafraid
    As though like me it gladly quitted
The shabby, shattered zones of fire
    With barbed wire webbed, with burnt scars pitted.

It was my hour, and sunset's flower;
    Now I could breathe and shed my trouble;
The track even here had danger in it,
    And the next farm lay a heap of rubble.

So being alone, my last job done,
    I followed the course of that lithe water
Westward in blossoming waywardness,
    Such beauty neighbouring so much slaughter,

With ray and song beguiled along;
    It seemed the war, for all its cunning,
Had missed this orchard brook, or some
    Especial fortune kept it running;

Half scared at this, something amiss,
    I doubted whether cursed illusion
Had seized my brain and lured me on
    To some intolerable conclusion;

So paused, went back to the general track,
    The safer way for soldiers' walking:
And as the stream's last murmur stilled,
    Our sixty pounders started talking.

Company Commander, 1917

'How lovely are the messengers that preach us the gospel of peace.'
So sang my friend, the company commander, in the trough of war,
Amid interminable shocks and snags, expecting no release.
It was not irony that prompted his song; though the daily score
Of casualities was even at the moment employing his pen,
And though his ridiculous shelter could stop no missile more
Than an empty bully-tin, being the target of daily torrents
Of hissing, shattering shells; yet no shell tore
Through VID.'s own armament; signing returns and warrants
He recalled old music, commanded, guarded, jollied his men.

'O for the peace that floweth like a river.'
That too he sang, and damned, at each pause, the red-tabbed Brigade,
Whose orders for grimness more than the frost-spell made us shiver;
Through VID.'s mild music loomed some bomb-and-bayonet raid.
Dead lies my friend, the fighter, from whom I have rarely heard
Against a human enemy one unhumorous word.

The Sum of All

So rise, enchanting haunting faithful
Music of life recalled and now revealing
Unity; now discerned beyond
Fear, obscureness, casualty,
Exhaustion, shame and wreck,
As what was best,
As what was deeply well designed.
So rise, as a clear hill road with steady ascension,
Issuing from drifted outskirts, huddled houses,
Casual inns where guests may enter and wait
Many a moment till the hostess find them;
Thence ever before the carter, passing the quarries,
The griffin-headed gateways,
Windmill, splashing rill, derelict sheepfold,
Tower of a thousand years –
Through the pinewoods,
Where warm stones lodge the rose-leaf butterfly;
Crossing the artillery ranges whose fierce signs
Mean nothing now, whose gougings look like
Bird-baths now; and last, the frontier farm
And guard-house made of bracken.
Rising to this old eyrie, quietly forsaken,
You bear me on, and not me only.
All difference sheds away,
All shrivelling of the sense, anxious prolepsis,
Injury, staring suspicion,
Fades into pure and wise advance.
So rise; so let me pass.

What is Winter?

The haze upon the meadow
    Denies the dying year,
For the sun's within it, something bridal
    Is more than dreaming here.
There is no end, no severance,
No moment of deliverance,
      No quietus made,
Though quiet abounds and deliverance moves
      In that sunny shade.

What is winter? a word,
    A figure, a clever guess.
That time-word does not answer to
    This drowsy wakefulness.
The secret stream scorns interval
Though the calendar shouts one from the wall;
      The spirit has no last days;
And death is no more dead than this
      Flower-haunted haze.

Timber

In the avenues of yesterday
A tree might have a thing to say.
 Horsemen then heard
 From the branches a word
That sent them serious on their way.

A tree, – a beam, a box, a crutch,
Costing so little or so much;
 Wainscot or stair,
 Barge, baby's chair,
A pier, a flute, a mill, a hutch.

That tree uprooted lying there
Will make such things with knack and care,
 Unless you hear
 From its boughs too clear
The word that has whitened the traveller's hair.

A Prospect of Swans

Walking the river way to change our note
From the hard season and harder care,
      Marvelling we found the swans.
The swans on sullen swollen dykes afloat
Or moored on tussocks, a full company there,
White breasts and necks, advance and poise and stir
Filling the scene, while rays of steel and bronze
From the far dying sun touched the dead reeds.

So easy was the manner of each one,
So sure and wise the course of all their needs,
So free their unity, in that level sun
And floodland tipped with sedge and osiery,
It might have been where man was yet to be,
Some mere where none but swans were ever kings,
Where gulls might hunt, a wide flight in from sea,
And page-like small birds come: all innocent wings.

O picture of some first divine intent,
O young world which perhaps was modelled thus,
      Where even hard winter meant
No disproportion, hopeless hungers none,
And set no task which could not well be done.
Now this primeval pattern gleamed at us
Right near the town's black smoke-towers and the roar
Of trains bearing the sons of man to war.

Thoughts of Thomas Hardy

'Are you looking for someone, you who come pattering
Along this empty corridor, dead leaf, to my door,
And before I had noticed that leaves were now dying?'

> 'No, nobody; but the way was open.
> The wind blew that way.
> There was no other way.
> And why your question?'

'O, I felt I saw someone with forehead bent downward
At the sound of your coming,
And he in that sound
Looked aware of a vaster threne of decline,
And considering a law of all life.
Yet he lingered, one lovingly regarding
Your particular fate and experience, poor leaf.'

The Vanishing Land

Flashing far, tolling sweet, telling of a city fine
The steeple cons the country round, and signals farm and kiln and
      mine,
Inns by the road are each one good, the carters here are friendly men,
And this is a country where I mean to come again and come again.
There was a child, though, last time I was passing by St Hubert shrine,
A child whose torn black frock and thin white cheek in memory
      brighter shine
Than abeles and than spires. I said, I pledge this blossom's better
      growth,
And so began, but one day failed; what sightless hours, and busy
      sloth
Followed, and now the child is lost, and no voice comes on any
      wind;
The silver spire gets farther off, and the inns are difficult to find.

The Tree in the Goods Yard

So sigh, that hearkening pasts arouse
In the magic circle of your boughs, –
So timelessly, on sound's deep sea,
Sail your unfurled melody,
       My small dark Tree.

Who set you in this smoky yard
None tells me; it might seem too hard
A fate for a tree whose place should be
With a sounding proud-plumed company
       By a glittering sea.

And yet you live with liking here,
Are well, have some brocade to wear,
And solitary, mysteriously
Revoice light airs as sighs, which free
       Tombed worlds for me.

After the Bombing

My hesitant design it was, in a time when no man feared,
To make a poem on the last poor flower to have grown on the
    patch of land
Where since a grey enormous stack of shops and offices reared
Its bulk as though to eternity there to stand.

Moreover I dreamed of a lyrical verse to welcome another flower,
The first to blow on that hidden site when the concrete block
    should cease
Gorging the space; it could not be mine to foretell the means, the
    hour,
But nature whispered something of a longer lease.

We look from the street now over a breezy wilderness of bloom,
Now, crowding its colours between the sills and cellars, hosts of
    flame
And foam, pearl-pink and thunder-red, befriending the makeshift
    tomb
Of a most ingenious but impermanent claim.

From the Flying-Boat

Into the blue undisturbable main
    The blue streams flow,
    In time they flow
Out of chasms vaporous, spurs far-whitening, winding gorges
    Woven of snow;
    This height we gain.
The country enlarges.

There the mountain cloudland, and far at the verge
    Cliff-cloudlands upsurge;
Here, countless, an archipelago –
How the islands tower in their strength, quincunxes so
May confront such eyes as understand them, down below;

    And yet up here I hardly know,
So little is this brilliant change, although
It extends in kingdom bright, so fast we go
Into apparent eternity – but, truth is, all things flow.

And now I am mounted aloft and have taken a wing,
Into the blue undisturbable oceaning,
More prospect than pyramidal Egypt, or perhaps the mountains of
    the moon could bring,
    With whom shall we meet in this place?
    Why hides He His face?

The Halted Battalion

One hour from far returns: Each man we had
Was well content that hour, the time, the place,
And war's reprieve combining. Each good face
Stood easy, and announced life not too bad.

Then almost holy came a light, a sense,
And whence it came I did not then inquire;
Simple the scene, – a château wall, a spire,
Towpath, swing-bridge, canal with bulrush fence.

Still I, as dreamer known, that morning saw
The others round me taken with a dream.
I wonder since that never one of them
Recalls it; but how should they? We who draw
Picture and meaning are dreamless, we
Are sentinels of time while the rest are free.

High Elms, Bracknell

Two buds we took from thousands more
   In Shelley's garden overgrown,
   Beneath our roof they are now full-blown,
A royal pair, a scarlet twain
   Through whose warm lives our thoughts explore
   Back through long years to come at one
Which Shelley loved in sun or rain.

Fleeting's the life of these strange flowers,
   Enchanting poppies satin-frilled,
   Dark-purple hearts, yet these rebuild
A distant world, a summer dead*
   Millions of poppy-lives ere ours,
   And Shelley's visionary towers
Come nearer in their Indian red;

Not but some shadow of despair
   In this dark purple ominous
   From that high summer beckons us;
And such a shadow, such a doom
   Was lurking in the garden there.
   We could not name the incubus,
Save that it haunted Shelley's home.

Was it that through the same glass door
   With weary heart, uncertain why,
   But first discerning love can die,
Harriet had moved, alone and slow;
   Or Shelley in the moonlight bore
   The cold curt word Necessity
From poppies that had seemed to know?

*in 1813

Then tracing the lost path between
    The herbs and flowers and wilderness,
    Whose was the phantom of our guess
Drawn by that quiet deserted pond
    With little boat, now scarcely seen
    For tears or bodings? Whose distress
Darkened the watery diamond?

The Evil Hour

Such surge of black wings I never saw homing
Fast from a winter day's pale-gilt entombing
    Nor can the continent's entire woodland house them.
So many throats of known and unknown runnels
Shooting from thorny cliffs or poured through tunnels
    I never heard. Such rainstorm to arouse them
We in these parts yet bore not in such torrents,
Nor warring winds enraged so to abhorrence;
    The sun was laughed to scorn, his god-head pelted
With sharp bones wrenched from sylvan nature; flamed then
A lightning such, all other lightning (tamed then)
    Might be as honey, or kind balms slow-melted.
Then this sad evening, this echo of existence,
And what was near driven to enormous distance.

Young Fieldmouse

Beseechingly this little thing –
Strayed from deep grass and breezy scented Spring
Into undreamed perils which have struck it down
Already – here in the den of the town
Takes refuge and finds pause in your warm palms
And dares to peer about, till its terror calms.

There is no hope for such a mangled mite,
Whose life depends on what we cannot guess,
Or nourishment, or surgery; none the less
Indulge this child, this stranger with eye so bright,
So dim – so bright again, for love can do
Much, and the illusion is good (in its time) as true.

We try our makeshifts, one by one they pass;
It tries; but in the end, in the long green grass,
The infant body stiffens, and the frame
Of the universe, to us, dies a little with the same.

The Fond Dream

Here's the dream I love.
   Stay, old Sleep, allow me this
   Yet one moment, godlike bliss.
Here's the dream I love.

Tell us then that dream?
   O, it's nothing, nothing at all.
   But I was walking young and small
In a scene like a happy dream.

What especial scene?
   None especial: pure blue sky,
   Cherry orchards a brook runs by,
And an old church crowns the scene.

Only that? If so,
   All would be well; but dreams have changed.
   Dreamers are banished, joys estranged.
I wake; it is not so.

C.E.B.

Ob. November 1951

Are all your eighty years defined at last
In so few terms? the chair and bookshelves by,
The latest pipe, the cared-for shoes, the stick
(Long since presented with some public thanks)
As good as new, but latterly less astir;
The post and railway times penned as of old
Beautifully for the fireside wall?
Not even your cricket-bag attending now,
Not the bream-ledger, nor the hop-ground picture,
Nor one school register, nor book of chants,
Though these will come to hand as days press on,
When your monastic face that seemed to pass
In a high procession from our local world,
Set on some boyhood vision, never uttered
To any but one, will be but village clay.

At the Great Wall of China

Perched in a tower of this ancestral Wall,
Of man's huge warlike works the hugest still,
We scan its highway lashing hill to hill,
We dream its form as though we saw it all;
Where these few miles to thousands grow, and yet
Ever the one command and genius haunt
Each stairway, sally-port, loop, parapet,
In mute last answer to the invader's vaunt.

But I half know at this bleak turret here,
In snow-dimmed moonlight where sure answers quail,
This new-set sentry of a long dead year,
This boy almost, trembling lest he may fail
To espy the ruseful raiders, and his mind
Torn with sharp love of the home left far behind.

A Hong Kong House

'And now a dove and now a dragon-fly
Came to the garden; sometimes as we sat
Outdoors in twilight noiseless owl and bat
    Flew shadowily by.
It was no garden, – so adust, red-dry
The rock-drift soil was, no kind root or sweet
Scent-subtle flower would house there, but I own
    At certain seasons, burning bright,
    Full-blown,
Some trumpet-purple blooms blazed at the sun's huge light.'

And then? Tell more.
'The handy lizard and quite nimble toad
    Had courage often to explore
    Our large abode.
The infant lizard whipped across the wall
To his own objects; how to slide like him
Along the upright plane and never fall,
    Ascribe to Eastern whim.
The winged ants flocked to our lamp, and shed
Their petally wings, and walked and crept instead.

'The palm-tree top soared into the golden blue
    And soaring skyward drew
Its straight stem etched with many rings,
And one broad holm-like tree whose name I never knew
Was decked through all its branches with broidering leaves
Of pattern-loving creepers; fine warblings
And gong-notes thence were sounded at our eaves
By clever birds one very seldom spied,
Except when they, of one tree tired,
Into another new-desired,
Over the lawn and scattered playthings chose to glide.'

Millstream Memories

Shattering remembrance, mercy! Not again
Could I delight in the child-bright scenes you wake.
Avoid, and quit my sight. Yet no: maintain
Whatever at last may guard me from the lake
Of darkness; dare not quit me, – stay, destroy
Some schemes and works which warped as time moved on;
Even the small pebble-songs bring rippling joy
Anew where later joy dropped woe-begone.
Gleam at my falling-off, assail my strength,
Deny my true love by far waters: she
Can understand, and all comes true at length, –
Your water-music teaches us to be.
I feared your elemental call, cool, light,
Leaf, life in the pearl? no more: shatter me quite.

Dog on Wheels

This dog – not a real dog, you know –
An Airedale, on four wheels, –
Not *my* toy, but a friend of mine as things go,
Is alone; we leave to the rest their reels.
I speak to him, he seems to hear.
His face is a little battered now,
And so is mine: to Change both bow.
Let that be: with vision I dream to endow
This dog on wheels.
                    Poor dear,
Can such things be? Not so.
We are simple, and that uplifted face
Is of its own kind in time and space.
But as I shut my desk and say goodbye,
Downward droops a disappointed eye.

And Away

I sent her in fancy,
For the pastime of pursuing,
Wherever old Time had been
  Kind to me;
By snow-enchanted woodlands,
Valley orchards, river windings,
Ancient tracks through hill cornfields,
  Ahead smiled she.

I set her in fancy,
If I might go and greet her
By guildhalls and minsters,
  By canal, by quay,
With hymns from glittering belfries,
With tunes from toying cafés,
Flower-markets, flower-costumes,
  Away explored she.

I thought she might laugh and
Rejoice, should I suddenly
Stand by her undecided
  In a far countree.
I was ghostly or dreaming,
Travelling all the long miles there.
I asked her to know me.
  'Elsewhere,' stared she.

Darkness

The fire dies down, and the last friend goes,
The vintage matters no more now;
Tomorrow's development no man knows,
But that we have faced before now;
    The night comes on apace.

Darkness. Our revels, if that name serves,
Are ended. Now for the battle of nerves.
The embers cool, the jokes turn sour,
The local's lost, and hugest power
    Comes prowling round the place.

But that's not new: there are older men
Who have been through that again and again –
There are children who will live to tell
The story of our stupid hell
    To a fresh and charming race.

For whom the night shall never need
Our smoky shelterings, day succeed
Unpresaged with our wilful moods
Transformed into enormous broods
    Of horror in dreadful chase.

Early 1941

A Swan, A Man

Among the dead reeds, the single swan
Floats and explores the water-shallow under,
While the wet whistling wind blows on
And the path by the river is all alone,
And I at the old bridge wonder
If those are birds or leaves,
Small quick birds or withered leaves,
Astir on the grassy patch of green
Where the wind is not so rough and keen.

What happens to my thought-time,
To my desires, my deeds, this day?
The rainstorm beats the pitiful stream
With battle-pictures I had hoped to miss
But winter warfare could be worse than this;
Into the house, recall what dead friends say,
And like the Ancient Mariner learn to pray.

Ancre Sunshine

In all his glory the sun was high and glowing
Over the farm world where we found great peace,
And clearest blue the winding river flowing
Seemed to be celebrating a release
From all but speed and music of its own
Which but for some few cows we heard alone.

Here half a century before might I,
Had something chanced, about this point have lain,
Looking with failing sense on such blue sky,
And then become a name with others slain.
But that thought vanished. Claire was wandering free
Miraumont way in the golden tasselled lea.

The railway trains went by, and dreamily
I thought of them as planets in their course,
Though bound perhaps for Arras, how would we
Have wondered once if through the furious force
Murdering our world one of these same had come,
Friendly and sensible – 'the war's over, chum'.

And now it seemed Claire was afar, and I
Alone, and where she went perhaps the mill
That used to be had risen again, and by
All that had fallen was in its old form still,
For her to witness, with no cold surprise,
In one of those moments when nothing dies.

3 September 1966

'Going over the ground again': the poetry of witness

Autumn in the evening and the morning now, and I can't keep the war out – 10 years ago the deluge, and no doubt if it was one hundred the character of the Somme scenery and those British attempts and works would still be distinct.[1]

Thus Edmund Blunden to his friend Siegfried Sassoon in 1926, ten years after setting foot in France as a soldier in the Royal Sussex Regiment. This selection is published a hundred years after the end of the First World War, and if the 'Somme scenery' and 'British attempts' are still distinct to readers, it is due in part to the powerful works of writers such as Blunden and Sassoon. They are both among the 16 war poets commemorated on one stone in Westminster Abbey; of that company, Blunden and David Jones served the longest at the Front, both dying in 1974.[2] Their longevity allowed them to see the beginning of a revival of interest in the war poets, a revival that left their work overshadowed by the bright star that Wilfred Owen has become, and by the more immediately engaging ironies and anger of Sassoon. This selection aims to restore Blunden to his place as a deeply thoughtful poet of war and peace, a poet of remembrance: a survivor who was a significant member of what the historian Jay Winter calls 'the first… "generation of memory" in the twentieth century.'[3]

In this essay I am drawing on recent critical writing about the poetry of the First World War, as well as cultural studies of memory and trauma in that war, in order to set Blunden's poetry in a more complex and illuminating context than that which was available in 1982, when I first edited his selected poems. The discussion of war writing was then dominated by Paul Fussell's study *The Great War and Modern Memory* (1975), which remains a key critical text. Fussell is an eloquent and sympathetic commentator on *Undertones of War*, calling it 'an extended pastoral elegy in prose'. He quotes the poet G.S. Fraser's judgement that it was 'the best war *poem*', which Fraser sought to demonstrate by printing excerpts as free verse in the *London Magazine*.[4]

Blunden derived his understated authority as a pastoral poet from his boyhood in Kent:

[…] it was hardly possible for any of us not to know something of our three rivers, each differing in character, of our hopfields and orchards and sheepfolds, and much else that was apparently eternal. If I wrote eagerly of these things it was not because I was following […] 'The Georgians' […] but because my themes were daily experiences.[5]

In 1916 he managed to publish several small, privately printed collections of poems, declaring his regional loyalties in the preamble to *Pastorals*: 'I sing of the rivers and hamlets and woodlands of Sussex and Kent'; his literary ones in the dedication of *The Barn* to Leigh Hunt (whose biography he was to publish in 1930) and of *Three Poems* to John Clare.[6] These collections were to be his calling-cards after the war, when he approached Siegfried Sassoon, then literary editor of the *Daily Herald*, and John Middleton Murry, editor of the *Athenaeum*. Both editors felt they had made a discovery; Sassoon had grown up in the same landscape as Blunden:

> Here was someone writing about a Kentish barn in a way I had always felt but never been able to put into verse. I forgot that I was in a newspaper office, for the barn was physically evoked, with its cobwebs and dust and sparkling sun, its smell of cattle cake and apples stored in hay, the sound of the breeze singing in the shattered pane and sparrows squabbling on the roof.[7]

> > Rain-sunken roof, grown green and thin
> > For sparrows' nests and starlings' nests;
> > Dishevelled eaves; unwieldy doors,
> > Cracked rusty pump, and oaken floors,
> > And idly-pencilled names and jests
> > Upon the posts within…

Affectionately precise observation is the mainstay of 'The Barn', but it is also the narrative of a supernatural visitation that has disastrous consequences for the farm. Later Blunden would not draw such explicit morals; what persisted, though, was his intuition of unease, a sense of lurking, malign spirits. (In this he resembles Walter de la Mare, whom he admired.) At home in England, he saw very clearly signs of distress, decay and destruction in the countryside, as well as its idyllic aspects; from the trenches, the countryside behind the lines could be 'a relaxed, non-resisting landscape that continually offers [the soldier] the picturesque, never the problematical'.[8] 'And where I stand the road is rippled over / With airy dreams of blossomed bean and clover', Blunden observes, for example, in 'Bleue Maison' (p.8). His war experience, paradoxically, offered 'delight' equal to that found in his childhood landscapes. With deep fellow-feeling for the Gloucestershire poet Ivor Gurney, he wrote in the introduction to Gurney's poems:

> The country close to the line [in the summer of 1916] was still very little harmed; its husbandry remained quietly perfect; its substantial towns, villages, lonely corners, field-side shrines, avenues, villas, brooks and canals, beneath blue and white skies, and in dewy midnights, were peace itself – and more than common peace to those who found themselves alive and respited for a space. The inhabitants were going on their ways as calmly as if the war was a greater distance off than an hour's walk, and the ordered life of centuries of good sense could be seen all around.[9]

What does it mean to say, then, that Blunden was a 'pastoral poet', relying on what Fussell calls 'arcadian recourses'?[10] It means more than describing fields and fish, barns and birds. Blunden served two years at the Front, 1916 to 1918, which included the battles of the Somme and Passchendaele. At the end of *Undertones of War* he presents himself as a 'harmless young shepherd in a soldier's coat', and the shepherd is of course the prime pastoral figure, whose life is defined by its simplicity, its disengagement from the world of getting and spending; it is the very opposite of martial. The shepherd's twin brother is the amateur fisherman, described by Isaak Walton in *The Compleat Angler* (1653) – a book Blunden knew from childhood – as a man 'of mild, and sweet, and peaceable spirits'.[11] The classical pastoral depicted a stable world, a world of work, friendship and song, yet it was not without melancholy, because entwined with elegy for that world, disappearing or already lost. As a distinct place, or emblematic of a 'Golden Age', the Arcadia of the famous epigraph *Et in Arcadia ego* is a thing of the past, whether the phrase is interpreted as 'I, too, once lived in Arcadia' or 'Even in Arcadia, I, death, hold sway'. This rich literary hinterland for the figure of the shepherd is further complicated by the Romantic reaction against what had become by the 18th century a more decorative tradition. In Wordsworth's *Prelude* he is 'A solitary object and sublime': a shepherd not bathed by Mediterranean sunshine but battling snow and winds in Cumbria.[12]

There is, therefore, a recognised tradition in which a poet might place himself as 'shepherd', and hold on to that as both literary standard and lived experience. For Blunden, there was a child-hood Arcadia in the gentler landscapes of Kent and Sussex, 'village England'; here was a felt and vital continuity with a life close to that of previous generations.[13] 'Almswomen' (p.9), 'Forefathers' (p.23) – these poems from the 1920s memorialise rural ways of life ruptured by the First World War. Sassoon greatly admired 'Almswomen', 'The Pike' and 'Perch-Fishing' but wrote, on receiving *The Waggoner*, 'for God's sake don't let them make you into a professional Georgian.'[14]

It has been easy to relegate Blunden to the Georgian ranks, forget-ting how the Georgian poetry anthologies edited by Edward Marsh in 1912 and 1915 once 'implied vigour, revolt and youth', even if after 1917 they suggested 'retrenchment, escape and ennervation'.[15] Certain critics did make an exception of Blunden in their dismissal of what T. S. Eliot called the 'rainbows, cuckoos, daffodils and timid hares' school (*Egoist*, March 1918), a watered-down pastoralism, but when Middleton Murry complained that there was 'nothing disturbing' about the Georgians (*Athenaeum*, December 1919), he ignored exactly that element in Blunden's poetry, as in other poetry that appeared under this convenient label.

In her thought-provoking essay 'War Pastorals', Edna Longley writes:

> As English people became the most town-based in Europe, there was a surge of cultural compensation: a back-to-nature move-ment; renewed attention to all forms of folk tradition; ideological investment in country life, 'village England' and the vanishing farm-labourer as bearers of national identity. [Edward] Thomas belonged to this cultural tendency.[16]

She points out that Thomas's poems also admit 'omens from wild nature. Wind, rain, and other waters often symbolize Thomas's sense that human beings do not control their environment, cannot read it, cannot control themselves'.[17] Thomas was writing poetry in the last three years of his life, in his late thirties, after decades of earning his living through reviewing and writing dozens of books and articles; he was already a mature writer. Blunden's poetry in *The Waggoner* (1920) and *The Shepherd* (1922) was the work of a man in his mid-twenties, deeply rooted in the English countryside and then uprooted by a war he first encountered as a teenage officer, sieved through a sensibility soaked in poetry: classical, Metaphysical, Augustan, Romantic – not to forget traditional ballads and Shakespeare. He loved the worked landscape of his home counties but, like Thomas, he understood and had seen what was uncontrollable in nature and man.

Therefore these early volumes are not entirely a picture of the countryman 'in clover'. In 'Sheet Lightning' (p.26) the distant storm and pent-up heat loose tongues and violence; the millstream wreaks its vengeance in more than one poem. The pike is a 'murderous patriarch'; the 'immemorial bream' plan 'the doom of man'; the 'orts' of snake, kite and stoat hang from fences; and on a windy November morning the beggar 'leaves the last of many homes – / Where mouldered apples and black shoddy lie'.

Moreover, the metaphors of war leach back into these poems of peace. 'The Pike' (p.11) is an example: the weir has 'bastions' and its apparent calm is destroyed by the fish's sudden, murderous offensive. The wind in 'Spring Night' blows 'So mad... so truceless and so grim / As if day's host of flowers were a moment's whim' (p.25). The familiar 'host' would go unnoticed except that the striking 'truceless' alerts us to its original military connotation; soldiers' lives as brief as flowers are subject to the scythe. In 'Perch-Fishing' (p.17) a boy's angling skills are eclipsed by Blunden's transfer of sympathy to the bereft mate, thinking of 'a thousand things the whole year through / They did together, never more to do'. The human lament for slain comrades is palpable; the agony persists. These are early days yet for a subject that he never leaves behind.

The inability to separate out peace from war is not unique to Blunden. Longley points out the same entanglement in the poetry of Ivor Gurney, a more damaged survivor, starting from his first collection, *Severn and Somme* (1917).

> The issue of pastoral and war is not confined to whether invocations of rural landscape figure naively as nostalgia or knowingly as irony. What matters is the ability to hold pastoral (the sum of literary negotiations with Nature) and war in the same frame. [...] Nonetheless, Blunden's retrospects belong to the transference whereby [Rosenberg's] 'torn fields of France'... also signify a violated England and violated English pastoral, while the trenches haunt the English landscape.[18]

As the years wore on, the challenge of holding these two elements in the same frame did not diminish for Blunden.

In his study of the genre, Marinelli suggests that 'Essentially the art of pastoral is the art of the backward glance, and Arcadia from its creation the product of wistful and melancholy longing. The pastoral poet reverses the process (and the "progress") of history.'[19] Longley extends this perception by arguing that the over-arching genre of Great War poetry is elegy, against Eliot's contention that there were only two kinds of war poetry, 'Romance' and 'Reporting',[20] and elegy of course mourns what is lost. What is lost in war is not only the youth of the boy soldiers, but also many of the friendships made by war. Blunden's loyalty to these was unswerving. The loyalty was reciprocated: at his funeral, a wreath of Flanders poppies was placed on his coffin by his runner from Ypres and Passchendaele, Private A.E. Beeney.

Blunden's war losses were compounded in 1919 by the death of his first child at only forty days. He had married Mary Daines very soon after meeting her in 1918; she was one of thirteen children of a village blacksmith, and only eighteen years old. In an unpublished autobiographical essay, he wrote that 'Anything more remote from the army life in which I had been submerged for some years could not be imagined [...] the rows of brick cottages without a shellhole in their roofs or in their gardens, the church and the clockface on the tower.'[21] 'In a Country Churchyard' (p.70), one of several elegies to his first daughter, presents death as change, motion; the formal stanzaic pattern – like the deceptively unyielding church tower – barely controls the agitation beneath:

So lies thy skull? This earth, even this
　Like quicksand weaves.
Sleep well, my darling, though I kiss
　Lime or dead leaves.

With the despairing 'even this', Blunden implies a similarity between the churchyard and the burial grounds he had known, where ample use was made of quick-lime to hasten decomposition and conceal the stench.[22] All creation is subject to the same 'deadly flowing'.

Blunden found that he could not settle to an academic life and left Oxford; like Thomas before him, he became a literary journalist. He edited, with Alan Porter, 150 *Poems Chiefly from Manuscript* by John Clare (1920), the first publication of 90 of the poems. Robert Graves, with whom he had become friends in Oxford, felt that Blunden's identification with the 19th-century poet was dangerous to his mental equilibrium:

He represents to you the victim of village life, unsuccessful in his attempts to win recognition in spite of the help given him by Old Blues on the *London*. Where Clare failed you are out to succeed and thus avenge him. You have avenged him most miraculously and restored him to popular recognition.[23]

Blunden's introduction to the edition suggests that their similarities went further than their village origins, precision of observation and an underlying faith – sternly tried in both men – in some principle of order. He remarks that 'imagination, colour, melody and affection were Clare's by nature,' but that 'sometimes his incredible facility in verse […] was not his best friend'. The intimacy with Clare's work led Blunden to write 'The Death Mask of John Clare', which despite its evocation of the asylum years is resolutely serene, and its antithesis, 'Clare's Ghost' (p.20). Here peace is pitched out, the wild night calls up and embodies all the restlessly uncompromising aspects of genius: 'deathless discontent'.

He was teaching in Japan by the time he published his third post-war collection, *Masks of Time*, in 1925. Blunden declared that its second section brought together 'some verses relating to war experience and its reverberations, verses intended to take their place in a series which should be a comprehensive view of their great and strange subject, in so far as the author is fitted to give it'. The note of modesty was absolutely characteristic of the man,[24] but the ambition was clear. Having tried to set down his experience in prose immediately after the war, and abandoned it, he embarked on writing *Undertones of War* in Tokyo, with a couple of maps as his only reference points. The novelist and war veteran H.M. Tomlinson, when he reviewed the memoir, called it a book 'by a ghost for other ghosts'.[25]

Ten years after the ending of the First World War, there was a stream of memoirs and novels by 'other ghosts'. Blunden's was unique in its tone and in providing a 'Supplement of Poetical Interpretations and Variations', 31 poems beginning with 'A House in Festubert':

> It hived the bird's call, the bee's hum,
> The sunbeams crossing the garden's shade –
> So fond of summer! still they come,
> But steel-born bees, birds, beams invade.
>   – Could summer betray you?

where the materials of war are treacherously naturalised, and ending with unexpected nostalgia in 'The Watchers' (p.86):

When will the stern fine 'Who goes there?'
Meet me again in midnight air?
And the gruff sentry's kindness, when
Will kindness have such power again?

Blunden later added a poem to the second edition of *Undertones* (published in June 1930), 'Return of the Native', dated Ypres 1929. He echoes the title of Thomas Hardy's novel to indicate the extent of his ongoing exile from ordinary life, the impossibility of constructing a less costly relationship with the past that obsesses him. The poem has a Hardyesque tone, too, in its contemplation of the immutable aspects of land and weather despite man's attempt at intervention.[26] Nature has coolly reasserted itself over ground whose every inch had been contested:

Leaving us with this south-west breeze to whisper
In bushes younger than ourselves, and cool
Foreheads still touched with feverish wonderings
Of what was once Time's vast compulsion, now
Incapable to stir a weed or moth.[27]

Such reassertion is both comforting and chilling; can this be held in the same frame? 'The Unchangeable' (p.12), by its very title, suggests that they can: 'Though I within these last two years of grace / Have seen the bright Ancre scourged to brackish mire', it begins; 'Spite of all this, I sing you high and low, / My old loves, Waters...' the poet declares. It is not simply a matter of ironic contrasts, although they are made, or of judging that old conventions are entirely inadequate to the new situation. Value resides in the language itself. Invoking traditional forms (the opening of the *Aeneid*, for example, 'Arms and the man I sing...') in descriptions of trench warfare provided both a sense of continuity and a reminder of loss. Blunden's style of archaism, apostrophe, rhetorical questioning, and the personifications scattered throughout his texts – Love, Fancy, Decline – are not mere decoration, they are essential to his meaning. They can be dismissed as 'literary luggage'[28] (and certainly they sometimes strike the reader as excess baggage), but Fussell offers a spirited defence:

With language as with landscape, his attention is constantly on pre-industrial England, the only repository of criteria for measuring fully the otherwise unspeakable grossness of the war. [...]

Blunden's style is his critique. It suggests what the modern world would look like to a sensibility that was genuinely civilised.[29]

Blunden liked to acknowledge poetic ancestors and connect generations: there are echoes of Coleridge's poetry in Blunden's to the very last; and Coleridge himself was 'deep in the verse of [William] Collins', as Blunden pointed out in the introduction to his edition of Collins's poems in 1929. He found 'How Sleep the Brave' to be 'the most consoling and unstrained elegy for our dead in Flanders'; he did not attempt analysis, having learned to love Collins's poem 'under conditions which have tested poetic preference with searching and tyrannous insistency'. Edna Longley comments that poets' 'war letters and diaries abound in incidental canon-making': Gurney singling out Milton, Keats and Shakespeare; Owen adding to those Homer, Dante and Shelley; Rosenberg mentioning Homer and Whitman, alluding also to the Romantics in his work. Shakespeare, Blunden wrote later, 'knew very well what happens to men and round them in real war; he is exact in all points.'[30] Blunden and Thomas shared a love of Hardy (whom Owen regarded as 'potatoey'), and we see Blunden's indebtedness to Hardy in metrical and stanzaic patterns (for example, 'Familiarity', p.88) and also in his habit of attaching the negative prefix to words: 'undelight', 'uncreation', 'unpurposed', 'unmurdered'. Longley maintains that 'In Great War poetry, literary allusion becomes at once ironical, interrogative, and revisionary.'[31]

Modernist poetry is marked by its willingness to incorporate quotation, and Blunden could well have said with Eliot, 'these fragments I have shored against my ruins'.[32] His poems are seeded with quotation, but Modernism resides in a perceived disconnection, and Blunden's practice is to make the connections work hard, to embed fragments. It seems as though he has been carrying in his head the cadence of a remembered line, and then uses it, almost conversationally, to launch a poem, as in the opening of 'At Senlis Once' (p.60) with Milton's 'How comely it was, and how reviving…'.

A fine example is 'Vlamertinghe: Passing the Château, July 1917' (p.77). The title, as Jon Silkin remarked in his perceptive readings of Blunden's poems in Out of Battle, would be appropriate to some diary entry of a leisurely Grand Tour: here the soldiers' experience, those who 'live with death and lice', is contained within traditional sonnet form.[33] Yet the opening line taken from Keats's 'Ode on a Grecian Urn' – 'And all her silken flanks with garlands drest' – extends the experience immediately. Blunden's poem is an answer to the question raised in stanza four of the 'Ode': 'Who are these coming to the sacrifice?' There Keats's wondering spectator composes an origin for the sacrificial procession, sees a town deserted in the stasis of art: 'and not a soul to tell / Why thou art desolate, can e'er return'. In Blunden's poem there may indeed be no return for the soldiers going up the line, prematurely and incongruously set among flowers, offering their own reproof to the poetry dressing nature in 'damask' and 'vermilion'. Here, the juxtaposition of flowers and war, so often remarked on as to become almost banal in accounts of the Great War, gains from Keats's presence in the first line. The famous last lines of 'Ode on a Grecian Urn' – 'Beauty is truth, truth beauty,– that is all / Ye know on earth, and all ye need to know' – gives the soldiers and the flowers a symbolic power that complicates the relationship between truth and beauty in such a setting. Blunden has returned, to speak of sacrifice and desolation. The jarring 'mate' in the penultimate line reminds us of the comradeship he reaches for as a survivor; there is even a touch of anger in that intonation.

While Blunden could not be called a Modernist poet by any stretch of that term, critics have pointed out the ways in which the war poets had modernity thrust upon them. Sarah Cole, in her discerning exploration of male friendship in the Great War, argues that the war poets

> tend to have a slightly equivocal status in modernism – canonical yet a little off-centre, in the sense that their texts tend not to perform the kinds of radical experimentation often valorised in and as modernism.[34]

In prose, Blunden acknowledged how difficult it was to hold the experience together:

> Towards Hooge one brazen morning, running in a shower of shells along 'The Great Wall of China' [...] Kenward the corporal and I saw a sentry crouching and peering one way and another like a birdboy in an October storm. He spoke, grinned and shivered; we passed; and duly the sentry was hit by a shell. So that in this vicinity a peculiar difficulty would exist for the artist to select the sights, faces, words, incidents which characterised the time. The art is rather to collect them, in their original form of incoherence.
> (*Undertones*, Chapter XVIII)

King Lear, to which he alludes again and again ('my perpetual great poem' [35]), has just this challenge of incoherence at its core. Poetry provided a coherence and order that were vital to Blunden: ballads, sonnets, iambic pentameter, a variety of quatrains, regular rhymes— all these were links with tradition, were testament to the poet's ability to control and contain what was otherwise formless and uncontrollable. John Greening, arguing that 'Third Ypres' (p.38) is Blunden's greatest poem, sees it as a battle for poetic style:

> It is just as much the enactment of mental collapse as *The Waste Land*, but where Eliot adopts a new scale, a new language ensemble, Blunden clings to the old octave, believes in tonality and the traditional musical forces.[36]

This choice was partially responsible for his falling out of fashion in the 1930s. Back in England, he found disfavour with the critics. Michael Roberts, whose *Faber Book of Modern Verse* (1936) shaped the taste of a generation or more, excluded him from the anthology (along with Edward Thomas) as one of those who had written good poems but had not 'been compelled to make any notable development of poetic technique'.[37] In *New Bearings in English Poetry*, F.R. Leavis had dealt with this point in praising Blunden's distinctive poise: 'He was able to be, to some purpose, conservative in technique and to draw upon the eighteenth century, because the immemorial rural order that was doomed is real to him.' Leavis, however, censured Blunden's more recent poetry for being on the one hand too hospitable to 'nymphs and their attendant classicalities' and on the other, too directly descriptive of his 'unease, his inner tensions, instead of implying them, as before, in the solidity of his created world.'[38] Perhaps, with over 300 pages of *Poems 1914–1930* before him, in a thematic arrangement, it was not easy to see how distinctive Blunden's expression of unease in his solid but haunted world remained.

In the present selection, the war predominates as it did in Blunden's own life. That he could write graceful, playful poetry is evident – as in the poems here from *Choice or Chance* and *An Elegy*, for example – and that he could write poetry of sudden illumination, of solace in nature, as in 'The Kiss' ('I am for the woods against the world') and in love ('The Surprise'). There were poems in the 1930s that paid homage to the poets he loved, and poems rejoicing in books and cricket. Nevertheless, there was the long shadow of the approaching war.

The Great War had only recently been allotted its unassailable ground, in the sense that the war graves were by then in their immaculate order. In 1936 Blunden had been asked to join the Imperial War Graves Commission, in succession to Rudyard Kipling, and he regularly went back to the battlefields and cemeteries. Blunden later wrote the foreword to a history of the Commission, and said he saw the cemeteries as a commemoration of those who had 'died for their friends' and that they were 'in a sense the poetry of that action'.[39] All he desired was that there should not be another war, and thus his visits to Germany, his close relationship with his German sister-in-law, inclined him to take a naively positive view of Hitler's rise to power, and to say so.[40] By mid-1940 he was back in uniform, with an honorary commission in the Oxford OTC, and instructing soldiers in map-reading. One of his pupils at Merton was Keith Douglas, an Old Blue to whom he became a mentor despite their very different temperaments and styles, as keen to get to a war as Blunden was to avoid one. He was killed by an exploding shell in Normandy in 1944, aged 24. The older man was convinced, as he wrote to Douglas, that 'the fighting man in this as in other wars is at least the only man whom truth really cares to meet.'[41]

In his 1928 essay on 'Siegfried Sassoon's Poetry', Blunden had written about the 'searing colloquial verses of desperation' in *Counter-Attack*, published in May 1918.

> In these Satanically laughable conditions of human misunderstanding (and here I write from a particular hatred of the period and the agonies of the Passchendaele illusion), a poet was found with the strength of mind to sacrifice everything, even the traditions of poetry [...] in order that he might make audible and intelligible in England and elsewhere the weeping Truth:

> > He went and said it very clear,
> > He went and shouted it in their ear.[42]

Blunden's formulations of the relationship of truth to combat experience, and thus to the writing that comes out of war, touches on a critical issue: are the 'truth of war' and the 'truth of poetry' compatible? Is there a 'true war poetry'? Douglas mulled over these questions in 'Poets in this War', in 1943. Hell 'was let loose in the Great War and it is the same old hell now', he wrote:

> The hardships, pain and boredom; the behaviour of the living and the appearance of the dead, were so accurately described by the

poets of the Great War that every day on the battlefields of the western desert – and no doubt on the Russian battlefields as well – their poems are illustrated. Almost all that a modern poet on active service is inspired to write would be tautological. [...] Their experiences they will not forget easily, and it seems to me that the whole body of English war poetry of this war, civil and military, will be created after the war is over.[43]

So he is already thinking that the truth will emerge in retrospect; pragmatically, too, because 'the mobility of modern warfare does not give the same opportunities for writing as the long routines of trench warfare.' Not forgetting has not quite – given Douglas's energetic mindset – become an inability to forget.

Twenty years later, the discussion was revived with the publication of the *Collected Poems* of Wilfred Owen, edited by Cecil Day Lewis and reprinting Blunden's Preface to the 1931 edition, on which he had spent so much effort. Blunden wrote to Sassoon specifically about Philip Larkin's review. The younger poet maintained that because war poets were reactive to the circumstances in which they found themselves they could not be regarded as the highest practitioners of an art where the subject should be actively chosen: 'the first-rank poet should ignore the squalid accident of war: his vision should be powerful enough to disregard it... [war] is essentially irrelevant.'[44] This is an echo of W.B. Yeats and his notorious rejection of 'the trench lyric' from *The Oxford Book of Modern Verse* in 1936, dismissing Owen and other war poets on the grounds that 'passive suffering is not a theme for poetry'.

I was questioning Larkin's rule that we should, as 'first-rank poets,' leave out the war we are deeply discussing in poetry. Something is there, something strange occurs there – not in Utopia. Agreed that we must not crowd the communication with dictionary terms [...] Poems are surely moments of vision. I was back in Zillebeke and at Dikkebusch Vijver as I wrote the last sentence, and saw both in the gloom and the beauty of two calendars.[45]

'Poems are surely moments of vision': here is the truth of poetry, which can include but not be limited to 'trench realism'.[46] Such a poem is Blunden's 'Pillbox' (p.61), which is centred on an incident rendered in casual speech, yet includes the line 'the ship of Charon over channel bore him'. At once we feel its weight and relevance. The poet's art enables him to combine the classical image of crossing that deep river which separates a man from his living comrades with the moment's recognition that the soldier will not be ferried home across the English Channel with a lucky, 'blighty' wound. The soldier, literally scared to death, moves out of the day's news and joins the long line of the immemorial dead.

What Larkin did not take into account, although he did greatly admire Owen, was that the war, far from being 'a squalid accident' became a condition of mind for many participants and survivors, not a passing circumstance that would find its place in the continuum of a life. Continuity and discontinuity are central ideas in discussions not only of the pastoral but also of what we now call post-traumatic stress disorder. Undoubtedly Blunden suffered from trauma – or shell shock, as it was then labelled – after his service in the First World War. 'Shell shock' is defined by Jay Winter as 'a condition in which the link between an individual's memory and his identity is severed'; 'the sense of having an integral personality, one with a then and a now which flowed together, becomes uncertain because of what he has felt and seen.'[47] Winter suggests that shell shock 'is a theatre of memory out of control'; 'before' and 'after' the event of war is not a linear but a circular concept. Despite the anchor of his country childhood, Blunden was condemned to this circling, and it had become his poetic subject.[48]

Robert Graves omitted a passage about Blunden in the 1957 revision of his memoir *Goodbye to All That* (a book Blunden and Sassoon regarded as a betrayal of their war experience), referring to their conversations in Oxford in 1919:

> Edmund had war-shock as badly as myself, and we would talk each other into an almost hysterical state about the trenches. We agreed that we would not be right until we got all that talk on paper. He was first with *Undertones of War*.[49]

Graves was mistaken in thinking that it could all be made 'right' with one book, at least for Blunden. An element of control was provided by writing about the experience within the continuities provided by literary tradition, but the dreams never stopped,[50] and the asthma and the dependence on alcohol remained; his traumatic experience was never treated. His daughter Margi, writing about their family life, remembers that he often talked about the places and men:

> By the time I was a teenager I was familiar with the names Ypres, Poperinghe, Hill 60, Zillebeke, Festubert, Jacob's Ladder, etc.

And the men – Tice, Collyer, Vidler, Amon, Worley… So whilst I was living my teenage years in the colourful and beautiful environment of the colony of Hong Kong, at Sunday lunch he might be talking about Flanders. […] it was as if, like the Ancient Mariner, he could not help but speak about it […][51]

This is not simply reminiscence, it is inhabiting the experience, 'going over the ground again'. The psychiatrist W.H. Rivers, who was so important in the treatment of traumatised soldiers at Craiglockhart, the Edinburgh hospital where Sassoon and Owen first met in 1917, was convinced that narration, not repression, was the key to recovery: 'subliminal memories were worse, because they never let go.'[52] And yet 'narrative' was itself compromised by the experience, because it could not be absorbed into a clear 'then' and 'now' sequence. A poem such as 'The Branch Line' (p.113) shows how easily the pleasures of the present give way to the apprehensions of the past, which may also signal the future.

One of the many ironies of this formative experience was the attachment to it, consciously or unwillingly. It came back in dreams, as reproach, and as odd as it seems to us now, as security and happiness. If the reproach is connected with survival, the happiness comes with the reminders of comradeship and trust.[53] 'Reunion in War' (p.34) makes it plain that human relations, beyond those with fellow soldiers, could not touch a man – 'We had not met but a moment ere / War baffled joy' – and that surviving those comrades was, immediately after the war, a cause of terrible guilt: '[I] knew for all my fear to die / That I with these lost friends should lie' ('War Autobiography'). In Tim Kendall's terrific formulation, 'A war poem represents the partial victory of unholy joy over shame.'[54] The living poet is still able to create, although wracked by survivors' guilt: the lasting poem is built on dead men's bones.

The idea of being what the philosopher Avishai Margalit calls in *The Ethics of Memory* a 'moral witness' is pertinent here, a state that he defines as 'knowledge-by-acquaintance of suffering', separating the witness from the observer or the victim. The difficulty is that such a witness has 'to live in order to serve', establishing not only the facts but what it means to be marked by them. He describes not only the war itself, but the memory and effect of war. Such spokesmen belong to a group which has also been through the fire – thus Blunden's annual attendance at his battalion reunions, and his deep friendships with veterans, pre-eminently Sassoon; they provide what Margalit calls a 'thick identity', based on shared bonds.[55] Naming was crucial: soldiers' names and place names in the poems; dates, too – all the identifying tags, 'lest we forget'. Eric J. Leed, in his persuasive study *No Man's Land*, maintains that trench warfare provided 'an environment that can never be known abstractly or from the outside' and quotes Charles Carrington's brutal declaration: 'I could not escape from the comradeship of the trenches which had become a mental internment camp.'[56] The effort to make outsiders – non-combatants, new generations – understand is crucial to the moral witness, at the same time as it is felt to be an impossible task.[57]

This is key to Blunden's return to the subject, in the 1940s' poems such as 'Company Commander, 1917' (p.127), 'The Vanishing Land' (p.133), 'The Halted Battalion' (p.137). It is key to his work on Wilfred Owen's poems in 1930, and his editing of Ivor Gurney's poems, mostly from unpublished manuscripts, in 1954. Blunden visited Gurney at Dartford Asylum, and wrote self-revealingly about him in the context of the unharmed countryside close to the front line:

> Add to this that Gurney [...] was with men of his own shire, in whom a like tradition and similar ability were personified, and we may see how this passage of his life as a soldier became a deep delight to him. When we observe that with it were mingled the extreme horror and futility of his battlefield days and nights, we apprehend the whole force of the period as it fastened on his imagination; and this also became even a tyranny over his later poetry.[58]

Blunden wrote the widely read pamphlet on First World War poets published by the British Council in 1958, and the Foreword to Brian Gardner's influential anthology, *Up the Line to Death*, in 1964, among many such introductions. Dominic Hibberd suggested that as 'critic, editor and academic', Blunden 'probably had more influence than anyone on the modern view of 1914–18 verse'.[59] If he did not bring these poets before the reading public, he was unfaithful to the dead; not only to their suffering but also to their truths.

Blunden's most anthologised poem, 'Report on Experience' (p.94), which begins 'I have been young, and now am not too old; / And I have seen the righteous forsaken' was published when he was 33. For the next forty years he never let go of the whole experience – or, it never let go of him – as we see in his last poem. It is as a poet, surely, that he would wish to be remembered and deserves to be read: an English poet, particularly of Kent and Sussex, in love with the English language and its poetic traditions; a pastoral poet, who felt time and the seasons on his pulse as he looked over his shoulder, painted their passing beauties and their harshness; a soldier-poet, who has left us the truth of his remembrance of peace and war, those nearly inseparable experiences.

Robyn Marsack

Notes

SOURCES

These are the books referred to frequently in the notes, in shortened form by initials, title or author.

Other references to information or quoted matter are given in full in the notes.

Edmund Blunden, *The Poems of Edmund Blunden 1914–1930* (London: Cobden-Sanderson, 1930)
EB: notes made in Claire Poynting's copy of this collection, in ink; also later pencilled emendations, possibly made for a proposed 'selected poems'. The book is now held in the Blunden Collection of the Harry Ransom Center, University of Texas.

Edmund Blunden, *The Shepherd and other poems of peace and war* (London: Cobden-Sanderson, 1922)
EBS: notes made by EB in this volume; for background see http://www.edmundblunden.org/newsevent.php?newseventid=1162 (accessed 30 March 2018)

Edmund Blunden, *Fall In, Ghosts – selected war prose*, edited by Robyn Marsack (Manchester: Carcanet Press, 2014)

Edmund Blunden, *The Deceitful Calm, a new selection of poems*, edited by Rennie Parker & Margi Blunden (Holt: Laurel Books, 2006), with useful notes (**TDC**)

Edmund Blunden, *Undertones of War*, edited by John Greening (Oxford University Press, 2015), with extensive notes and an additional poetry supplement

Robert Bridges, 'The Dialectical Words in Edmund Blunden's Poems', Society of Pure English tract no. 5, 1921. See http://www.gutenberg.org/files/12524/12524-h/12524-h.htm (accessed 16 March 2018)

John Milton, *Poetical Works*, ed. Douglas Bush (Oxford University Press, 1969)

Carol Rothkopf, ed., *Selected Letters of Siegfried Sassoon and Edmund Blunden*, 3 vols (London: Pickering & Chatto, 2012)

Barry Webb, *Edmund Blunden: a biography* (New Haven, CT: Yale University Press, 1990)

Joseph Wright, ed., *English Dialect Dictionary...*, 6 vols (London: Henry Frowde, publisher to the English Dialect Society, 1898–1905)

Drafts and fair copies of some poems, along with other documents and photographs, may be found in the Blunden section of the First World War Poetry Digital Archive – http://ww1lit.nsms.ox.ac.uk/ww1lit/collections

1. Blunden in James Gibson, ed., *Let the Poet Choose* (London: George Harrap & Co., 1973), p.31.
2. *Selected Letters*, 1, p.288 (21 June 1930).
3. Blunden, 'Country Childhood' in Simon Nowell-Smith, ed., *Edwardian England 1901–1914* (London: Oxford University Press, 1964), pp.571–2.
4. Webb, *Edmund Blunden*, p.26.
5. 'Country Childhood', p.573.
6. Blunden, 'De Bello Germanico', *Fall In, Ghosts*, p.35.
7. *Undertones of War*, Chapter VIII; this was in August 1916.
8. According to Rupert Hart-Davis, Robert Graves described Blunden as looking like 'a cross between Julius Caesar and a bird'; Henry Williamson likened his handwriting to 'the flight and appearance of that gentle bird [the night-jar]' (Webb, pp.3–4).
9. Virginia Woolf was among the 35 guests at the dinner for Blunden on the eve of his departure, and noted in her diary for 12 March 1924: 'Blunden despairing, drooping, crow-like, rather than Keats-like. And did we really all believe in Blunden's genius? Had we read his poetry? How much sincerity was there in the whole thing?' (Virginia Woolf, *A Moment's Liberty: the shorter diary*, London: Pimlico, 1997, p. 179). She may be referring to Keats as a generic poet-figure; perhaps she may have heard, via Sassoon, of Hardy's opinion: 'Edmund Blunden flitted in and out of Max Gate, with his perennial topics of the past war, Christ's Hospital, cricket, and Keats; he won from Hardy the valued though hardly correct opinion that he had an air of Keats himself' (Robert Gittings, *The Older Hardy*, Harmondsworth: Penguin Books, 1980, p.271).

   There are various references to Blunden by Woolf in her diaries and letters; in 1929 he was at a party given by the Woolfs along with VW's nephew, Julian Bell. In her diary for 12 May 1929 Woolf refers to him as 'little Blunden, the very image of a London house sparrow' (*A Moment's Liberty*, p.259). In a letter to Vita Sackville-West on 13 November 1929, she recounts asking Bell who were the best living poets: 'He replied at once Vita and Blunden' (*A Reflection of the Other Person: the letters of Virginia Woolf 1929–1931*, London, The Hogarth Press, 1978, p. 108). Bell published a volume of poetry, *Winter Movement*, in 1930, and received 'a charming letter' from Blunden, who reviewed the book anonymously for the *Times Literary Supplement* in 1931 (Peter Stansky & William Abrahams, *Journey to the Frontier, Julian Bell and John Cornford: their lives and the 1930s*, London: Constable, 1966, p.71). Bell was to die in Spain in 1937, aged 29, when the ambulance he was driving was bombed by the Nationalists. Ironically, Blunden was one of five to have taken Franco's side when asked to declare himself in *Authors Take Sides on the Spanish Civil War*, compiled by his friend and fellow veteran Edgell Rickword (Charles Hobday, *Edgell Rickword: a poet at war*, Manchester: Carcanet Press, 1989, pp.194–5).
10. Blunden, 'War and Peace', *Fall In, Ghosts*, pp. 47, 46.
11. Eric J. Leed, *No Man's Land: combat and identity in World War I* (Cambridge University Press, 1979), p.113 quoting from C.E. Carrington, *Soldiers from*

the Wars Returning (London, 1965), p.252.

12. Edmund Blunden, *War Poets 1914–1918*, published for the British Council and the National Book League (Harlow: Longmans, Green & Co., 1958; reprinted with additions to the bibliography 1964, 1969), pp.33–4.

13. *Selected Letters*, 1, p.208 (20 December 1928).

14. Quoted by Webb, p.243.

15. 'Line upon Line', *The Mind's Eye*, p.112. Blunden wrote that 'the earliest enjoyment of pictures I can recall came from a brightly tinted Japanese piece of finches on a bough…', 'Country Childhood', pp.551–2.

16. Blunden, *Nature in English Literature* (London: The Hogarth Press, 1929), p.58. Field mice make a notable appearance in the midst of battle in 'Third Ypres': '(These / Calmed me, on these depended my salvation.)'

17. Webb, p.318. Blunden unexpectedly won the vote to be Professor of Poetry (succeeding Robert Graves) against Robert Lowell; the American poet wrote him a gracious letter of congratulation.

18. On the day he died, Sassoon read a letter from a soldier who had served with him as a 16-year-old on the Somme. Having heard Sassoon declare 'I mean to put up a really good show', his son wrote to the veteran that he felt sure 'the thoughts in his mind of the old days in the trenches helped him over those last few hours' (Max Egremont, *Siegfried Sassoon: a biography*, London: Picador, 2005, p.518). The Great War was there to the end.

19. Letter to Douglas quoted in Desmond Graham, *Keith Douglas 1920–1944 – a biography* (Oxford University Press, 1974), p.218n. The 'truth of war' and the idea of fighting poets as the only writers able to convey it are discussed in the essay 'Going over the ground again' at the end of this volume.

NOTES TO THE POEMS

p.1 'By Chanctonbury'

Written in 1915, first published in *Pastorals, a book of verses* (London: Erskine Macdonald, June 1916). Chanctonbury is a hill on the South Downs, in West Sussex. It is the site of a prehistoric hill-fort, Chanctonbury Ring, and used to be crowned with beech trees (mainly destroyed in the storms of 1987).

p.2 'The Festubert Shrine'

EB: It *was* a pretty little *chapelle*. Festubert had not many antiquities. But it had the air of a comfortable old village, with plenty of good trees and gardens.

EB writes wistfully in the Preface to *Poems 1914–1930* that he wishes he'd had other poems available to him when making his choice: 'the numerous pieces which I remember to have occupied and diverted me in the summer of 1917, while we were making ourselves ready to capture and consolidate the large extent of Belgium then borrowed by Germany. The labours of that summer, however, down to my neat transcripts of "ode, and elegy, and sonnet," vanished in the mud.' Webb lists 18 poems as surviving from the trenches, of which this is one.

p.3 'Thiepval Wood'

EB: At that moment, north of Ancre was comparatively calm. One watched the great commotion at the south side.

Another of the surviving trench poems. The scene is described in Chapter IX of *Undertones*.

Line 1: 'heavies' – heavy artillery

Line 4: 'slatting' – Wright gives 'to drip, run down; to beat against' as a Sussex usage.

p.4 '"Transport Up" at Ypres'

EB: This pleased George Maycock M.C., our Transport Officer.

In his essay 'Fall In, Ghosts', EB writes that Maycock 'dramatized, or enjoyed the dramatic in, the dreariest situations of the grey old confusion' (*Fall In, Ghosts*, p.84).

Line 3: EB – corrected to 'Boulevard Malou' and 'then' crossed out

Line 8: 'picric' – an acid used in explosives

p.5 'Les Halles d'Ypres'

This is one of EB's poems that survived from the trenches, and it is now on a plaque beside the Cloth Hall in Ypres. He recounts his first visit to Ypres in Chapter XV of *Undertones*: 'There was in the town itself the same strange silence, and the searing pallor of the streets in that daybreak was unlike anything that I had known.' He had 'longed to see Ypres', believing that it could not be as desolate as described, but 'The bleakness of events had found their proper theatre.'

p.6 'Clear Weather'

Greening points out that EB was near St Omer, where the Royal Flying Corps was based.

Line 2: 'glintering' – not given in Wright or other dialect dictionaries

Line 3: 'gas gongs' – gongs and bells were placed along the front line so that sentries could raise the alarm about gas attacks. The first significant German gas attack was at Ypres in 1915; by 1916 it was released through shells rather than cylinders, allowing it to carry further.

Line 10: EB – 'bandogs' crossed out and 'yard-dogs' pencilled in; a bandog is a working dog that guards and protects property

Line 15: the Albatros was a German biplane, whose use on the Western Front peaked in November 1917.

Line 19: 'maxims' – machine guns

p.7 'Trees on the Calais Road'

EB: In training… about May.

Webb suggests that this poem was written in June 1917 (*Edmund Blunden*, p.335).

Line 6: *Miserere* – 'have mercy'

p.8 'Bleue Maison'

EB: Again not far west of Saint Omer. There *is* a place called something like Bleue Maison, but I fancy I have got it a bit out of order. What beautiful moments of just *seeing* what the world was like, while awaiting what, God knows what.

Line 7: 'curlock' – variously spelt as 'curlick' and 'carlock', a type of wild mustard

Line 8: 'St Elmo's fire' – a weather phenomenon a bit like lightning, due to a gap in electrical charge, often associated with ships' masts or aeroplane wings

p.9 'Almswomen'

EB: Composed by way of filling in time at Deve Cottage; the old ladies were actual, and the poem was therefore appreciated when it was read, almost as soon as written down.

Deve was the family home of Blunden's first wife, in Suffolk, and the poem describes Mary's great-aunt and her friend (*TDC*).

The poem was dedicated to Nancy and Robert Graves, who were neighbours of Blunden on Boar's Hill, Oxford. Blunden's friendship with Graves was damaged by the publication of *Goodbye to All That* in 1929. Blunden wrote to Sassoon on first reading it: 'I don't think a worse *book* was ever flung together. His unreliability, obvious in all passages where I was able to test from my own information, destroys his war scenes. His self-importance and cold use and slaughter of others ruin the possible solace of a personality' (*Selected Letters*, 1, p.241).

Webb writes that the poem began as an 'exercise' in the manner of Pope or Goldsmith, and was printed both in the *London Mercury* and the *Nation*. Writing to Sassoon in 1921, EB remarks: 'I am awaiting a real inspiration and a poem as obviously commanding as (after so much notice) I feel "Almswomen" is. I can't say that it pleases me to the same extent as it does better judges' (*Selected Letters*, 1, p.18). He wrote to his mother in 1924: 'Why should all my poems be neglected in order that Almswomen may abound? O sentimental condition of humanity!' (Webb, p.115).

Line 19: EB glossed 'Esau's hands' in *The Waggoner* as 'old-fashioned creeping garden plants, shaped like starfish'; Robert Bridges commended his use of English country names for common plants.

Line 31: 'saracens' – an onslaught of hailstones (*TDC*)

p.11 'The Pike'

EB: Generalised – Cheveney, Heaver's Mill, etc.

Line 4: EB glossed 'elver-peopled' in *The Waggoner*: Young eels are fond of the silk-weed on old watergates, and the clefts in the masonry behind the weed.

Line 17: changed to 'waterpit shelving and dark' in *Poems 1914–1930*

p.12 'The Unchangeable'

Line 3: 'chace' – obsolete spelling of 'chase', in its meaning of unenclosed land set aside for breeding and hunting wild animals

Line 9: 'lags' – Wright explains this as a Sussex and Somerset term for 'a long marshy meadow usually by the side of a stream'.

In *Poems 1914–1930* the last line was changed to 'Dance to the bubbling brooks of elfin song'.

p.13   'A Waterpiece'

EB: This pool was one of several on the River Beult about 1909. My father had had some steps cut down to the edge, but only those who knew the way through the wood would find it.

Line 2: 'pearl-smooth' was dropped in *Poems 1914–1930*; EB – 'silent' pencilled as substitute

Robert Bridges was one of the founders of the Society of Pure English, and Poet Laureate from 1913 until his death in 1930. He was one of several poets living on Boar's Hill, Oxford, when EB lived there. In one of the Society's tracts he writes about *The Waggoner* (1920) because in it the 'element of dialectical and obsolescent words is very prominent':

> The poetic diction and high standard of [Blunden's] best work give sufficient importance to this procedure; and though he may seem to be somewhat extravagant in his predilection for unusual terms, yet his poetry cannot be imagined without them, and the strength and beauty of the effects must be estimated in his successes and not in his failures.
>
> In the following remarks no appreciation of the poetry will be attempted: our undertaking is merely to tabulate the 'new' words, and examine their fitness for their employment.

Line 6: '*Hobby-horse* as a local or rustic name for dragon-fly can have no right to general acceptance' (Bridges).

Line 13: 'idola' – plural of 'idolum', a phantom or insubstantial image

p.14   'A Country God'

EB: on leave, early 1918

Line 2: 'stolchy'

> *Stolchy* is so good a word that it does not need a dictionary. Wright gives only the verb *stolch* 'to tread down, trample, to walk in the dirt'. The adjective is therefore primarily applicable to wet land that has become sodden and miry by being *poached* by cattle, and then to any ground in a similar condition. Since *poach* is a somewhat confused homophone, its adjective *poachy* has no chance against *stolchy*. (Bridges)

This statement by Bridges is contradicted by the later general uncertainty over the meaning of the word. Google comes up with references to articles querying its use by W.H. Auden in a late poem, 'A Bad Night'; perhaps Auden used Wright's dictionary, or had even come across the word as used by Blunden.

Line 21: 'bergomask' – a rustic courtship dance; it is danced in *A Midsummer Night's Dream* (Act 5, Scene 1).

Line 24: 'brish' – to mow lightly or trim, according to *A Dictionary of the Kentish Dialect and Provincialisms in use in the County of Kent*, compiled by W.D. Parish & W.F. Shaw (Lewes: Farncombe & Co., 1898).

p.16   'In Festubert'

EB: I dreamed much, when I was allowed a short sleep at Festubert. My feelings were still at home, and there were some likenesses in the scene round me, if my old village had also been under bombardment. As for dreams, indeed some took me beyond the German lines into queer battles for farms with moats around them & heavily sandbagged ruins of village streets.

W.B. Yeats chose six poems by EB in his *Oxford Book of Modern Verse 1892–1935*, notoriously not including Owen and other war poets on the grounds that 'passive suffering is not a theme for poetry'. 'In Festubert' was included, along with 'Report on Experience'.

Line 4: EB – pencilled change to 'Of incident and memory'

Line 7: 'hizzing' is changed to 'whizzing' in *Poems 1914–1930*, however Bridges points out that '*hizzing* is an old word now neglected. Shakespeare has "To have a thousand with red burning spits / Come hizzing in upon 'em".—*Lear*, III. vi. 17., and there are other quotations in *OED*.' Bridges also picks up 'daps': 'This word is well known to fishermen and fowlers, meaning "to dip lightly and suddenly into water" but is uncommon in literature.'

Line 12: 'glinzy' – glossed by EB in *The Waggoner* as 'slippery'

Line 14: changed to 'Thieves break into a pyramid' in *Poems 1914–1930*

p.17 'Perch-Fishing'

EB: The 2 large perch were taken by me at Langridge's Pond, Yalding, & surprised Mr Langridge, who I think is still there – but the pond is nothing today.

G.W. Palmer was a mathematician at Christ's Hospital and President of the Grecians' Reading Society, whose members were encouraged to read modern authors such as Shaw, Stevenson and Conrad.

Line 10: tansies – a yellow flower from the daisy family, thought to be useful as an insect repellent because of its strong smell; in *Poems 1914–1930* this was altered to 'bennets' – Herb Bennet is a member of the rose family, also yellow, and common in hedgerows and woodland.

Line 40: 'river-shrimps' was replaced in *Poems 1914–1930* by 'straying greaves', i.e. bits of fat made into fish-bait.

p.20 'Clare's Ghost'

EB: Written in war surroundings, from Framfield memories.

Framfield was where the Blunden family lived for a time, while Blunden was at Christ's Hospital. He discovered Clare's poetry in Arthur Symons' edition, and later devoted a great deal of time to bringing Clare's poetry into print; the edition which he edited with Alan Porter, for example, brought to light 90 poems that were previously unpublished. This poem came back from the trenches, but EB's copy of Clare's poems – chosen as a school prize – did not; he reports that his friend the war artist Xavier Kapp went off with it in spring 1916 (*Undertones*, Chapter III).

p.21 '11th R.S.R.'

EB: How *happy* the battalion was in ordinary country places!

EBS: The Sussex soldiers were chiefly countrymen.

EB published 'A Battalion History' of the 11th Royal Sussex Regiment in *The Mind's Eye* (1934). The battalion was variously known as the 'First

Southdowns, otherwise Lowther's Lambs... composed principally of Sussex men'. Lieutenant-Colonel Claude Lowther raised three battalions in 1914, recruited from volunteers with officers from the regular army, and the 11th RSR was sent to France in March 1916. EB concludes his essay in a mood of wistful remembrance, with a quotation from Shelley: 'It is all so long ago now; and yet when I think of the 11th Royal Sussex on a winter evening, under all its ordeals or in any of its recreations, *Bare winter is suddenly changed to spring*' (*Fall In, Ghosts*, p.113).

p.23 'Forefathers'
EBS: written at Oxford, summer 1923
Line 29: changed to 'There is silence, there survives' in *Poems 1914–1930*.

p.24 'November Morning'
EB: Congelow again. The shoddy was for the hopgardens.
TDC explains that Congelow was a farm house just outside the village of Yalding (Kent), which the Blundens rented for a few years from 1904.
Line 5: changed to 'of sackclothed skies and cold unfruited grounds' in *Poems 1914–1930*.
Line 6: 'slats' changed to 'beats'; 'weazen' – shrivelled
Line 12: 'shoddy' – wool from shredded rags

p.26 'Sheet Lightning'
EB: Some notion of Yalding about 1910
EBS: Recollection of a cricket outing about 1906
Line 20: 'higglers' – in the *Dictionary of the Sussex Dialect and Provincialisms in use in the County of Sussex* (compiled by Revd W.D. Parish, Lewes: Farncombe & Co., 1875), the definition is 'a huckster – so called from higgling over his bargains'; more generally, a pedlar
Line 28: 'ribbands' changed to 'the bright scarf' in *Poems 1914–1930*

p.28 'Cloudy June'
EBS: On the road to Abingdon, Oxford
Line 21: 'yapping' replaced by 'barking' in *Poems 1914–1930*.
Line 22: 'wheeze and play' replaced by 'talk and play' in *Poems 1914–1930*.
Line 23: 'my swooned passions drown' replaced by 'passions in such night drown' in *Poems 1914–1930*.

p.29 'Mole Catcher'
EB: Once more, much was from Bert Daines's recipe for a good mole-catcher.

> Bert Daines was EB's brother-in-law from his first marriage. EB described Bert as 'a repository of Anglian anecdote, fable, dialect and wickedness. He would tell me with perfect contentment whatever he knew of country life and occupation...' (*TDC*)

EBS: objected to by J.M. Murry as being too true
John Middleton Murry was the editor of the *Athenaeum* 1919–21, a literary review that published the work of T.S. Eliot, Lytton Strachey and Virginia Woolf among others. He was also an Old Blue. Blunden sent him an article on John Clare, to which JMM responded enthusiastically – 'beau-

tifully written (in both senses)'; people were always struck by EB's elegant handwriting – and that encouraged him to send in some poems. JMM wrote excitedly to his wife, Katherine Mansfield: 'He sent me a little book of poems this morning. They are immature, but it's the right kind of immaturity: trying hard at big things: poetry full of the country and of nature. […] isn't that the real stuff? I'm sure it is. I think he's our first real discovery, and he comes from my school!' (Webb, p.116) KM was less impressed, but Murry went on to publish 'Molecatcher' in the *Athenaeum*, 9 July 1920.

p.30 'The Scythe Struck by Lightning'
EB: Worked up from an anecdote in an ancient magazine.
Line 11: 'And Elijah said unto Ahab, Get thee up, eat and drink, for there is a sound of abundance of rain' – 1 Kings 18:41.

p.32 'The Poor Man's Pig'
Line 5: 'fresh-peeled osiers' in *Poems 1914–1930*

p.33 'Behind the Line'
EB: Some of us were driven back by the world of peace and its puzzles to the company of the years of terror.
EBS: Liked by H.M. Tomlinson, a veteran well able to share the some-what strange fascination of 'sand-bagged rooms' etc.
The novelist and journalist H.M. Tomlinson (1873–1958) was literary editor of the *Nation*, which opposed the war, and had been an official war correspondent in France until 1917. His anti-war novel, *All Our Yesterdays*, was published in 1930. *Undertones of War* was dedicated to his brother, Philip Tomlinson.
Line 10: 'that strange with fire' in *Poems 1914–1930*
Line 11: 'pyramid-fosse' – a fosse-trench had a parapet made of the exca-vated earth; on the Loos battlefield, for example, 'Fosse 8' was a slag heap, which was somewhat pyramid-shaped.
Line 16: 'double storm' in *Poems 1914–1930*

p.33 'Reunion in War'
EB: Imagined, but based on some mood during leave.
EBS: imaginary, but spiritually truthful
Line 5: 'glebe' – land attached to a parish church; here, the path to the churchyard
Line 36: 'bullace tree' – a variety of plum
Line 52: 'cereclothed' – a cerecloth is a winding sheet for a corpse.
Line 57: altered to 'To trace with foolish fingers' in *Poems 1914–1930*
Line 59: 'twitch' – Wright gives this as 'couch grass', and notes that John Clare writes 'twitchy nest' in his poem 'To the Lark'. EB's use of dialect words was certainly sanctioned, as it were, by the example of Clare, whose poetry he edited and championed.

p.36 'A Farm near Zillebeke'
EB: Early 1917, farm near 'Vince Street', it had not long to wait.
EBS: In the Ypres Salient, March 1917. The 'farm' could not be approached by daylight.

He describes the scene in Chapter XVII of *Undertones*:

> From that point, two trenches went on to the firing line, and it depended on incident or instinct which one we took. Vince Street, the north one, was solidly made and commanded a pretty view of a farm called Dormy House, in the court of which a cart stood with a load of musty straw, scarcely to be considered extant.

Line 6: 'hame' – a curved bar holding a harness trace

p.37 'Festubert 1916' ['1916 Seen from 1921']

EBS: where I first entered the trenches

The more familiar (second) title was adopted in *Poems 1914–1930*.

Lines 8–9: EB plays on the description of the 12-syllable Alexandrine verse form, 'That, like a wounded snake, drags its slow length along' in Alexander Pope's *An Essay on Criticism*, II, line 156.

Line 12: changed to 'I seek such neighbours here' in *Poems 1914–1930*

Line 21: 'redoubt' – a fort outside the main defensive line, often temporary

Line 25: the site of the early poem 'The Festubert Shrine'

p.38 'Third Ypres'

EB: July 31, 1917 & the next day or two.

EBS: The huge & hopeless battle of 1917

This describes the involvement of the battalion in the Third Battle of Ypres, which he also recounts in Chapter XXI of *Undertones*. The 11th Royal Sussex were relieved on 3 August, having suffered 275 casualties on the first two days (i.e. over a quarter of its strength), including two of EB's old school friends. While EB and others survived the shelling of a pill-box, the HQ of the nearby 13th Royal Sussex battalion was hit and wiped out on 2 August.

Line 5: fascines were bundles of rods or brushwood used to strengthen trenches or lay paths across marshy ground

Line 10: 'sap' was replaced by 'hook' in *Poems 1914–1930*.

Line 16: 'setting themselves in array' – EB used 'Yea, how they set themselves in battle-array / I shall remember to my dying day', from John Bunyan's introductory verses to *The Holy War* (1682), as an epigraph to *Undertones*.

Line 17: 'fourms' was glossed by EB as 'hares' lurking-places' in *The Shepherd*.

Line 33: to 'plash' a hedge is to interweave branches and twigs to make a strong barrier.

Line 45: EBS identifies the runner as Wrackley (or Rackley); in *Undertones* Chapter XXI EB writes of his death, 'a sensitive and willing youth, just as he set out for the companies; struck, he fell on one knee, and his stretched-out hand still clutched his message.'

Line 70: 'pollard' – a tree that has had its top and some branches lopped off (pollarded) to encourage new growth

Line 86: 'sties' – although printed 'sites' in several editions, Greening seems correct in this reading, which also aligns with the draft, see http://

wwılit.nsms.ox.ac.uk/wwılit/collections/document/9409/9291 (accessed 15 March 2018)

Line 96: EBS notes that the doctor 'was afterwards killed in a similar occurrence, which I escaped by a few yards'.

Line 103 ff: John Lewis-Stempel points out that mice – as opposed to rats and lice – were generally regarded with sympathy by the soldiers and could be a trigger for 'comforting childhood memories', in *Where Poppies Blow: the British Soldier, Nature, the Great War* (London: Weidenfeld & Nicholson, 2016), pp.173–5.

Line 106: EBS identifies the sergeant as 'W. Ashford, killed in 1918'; EB writes of him affectionately as the person who introduced him to champagne; fearless and always smiling (*Fall In, Ghosts*, p.84).

Line 120: this becomes 'Still swept the rain' in *Poems 1914–1930*.

p.42 'Death of Childhood Beliefs'

EBS: Remembrances of Yalding, Kent – an ancient village full of hops and cherries

Line 2: 'sallows' – small willow trees

Line 20: EBS: 'And visions, as poetic eyes avow, Hang on each leaf, and swarm on every bough'

Here he slightly misquotes Thomas Gray's fragment which appears in a letter to Horace Walpole: 'While Visions, as Poetic eyes avow, / Cling to each Leaf, & swarm on ev'ry Bough' (Thomas Gray and William Collins, *Poetical Works*, edited by Roger Lonsdale, OUP, 1977).

Line 23: Defeated in the battle of Worcester in 1651, the future King Charles II hid in an oak tree during his escape to France. The 'Royal Oak' stood in the grounds of Boscobel House, Shropshire.

Line 31: Christians who made the pilgrimage to the Holy Land in the Middle Ages would bring back a palm leaf as a souvenir, referring to Christ's entry into Jerusalem when the road was carpeted with palms.

Line 33: King David, to whom authorship of many of the biblical Psalms is ascribed

Line 37: a will o' the wisp in British folklore is both a ghostly light that leads travellers astray, and the spirit who holds the light.

Line 55: Armageddon in the New Testament is the last battle between good and evil before the Last Judgement; used more generally for apocalyptic conflict.

p.44 'The Canal'

EBS: At the same place [Yalding]. The metre altered from Campion's 'Rose cheek'd Laura'.

Verses 9 &10 Several suicides by drowning occurred in this canal, or the similarly sullen Medway near it.

Thomas Campion (1567–1620) wrote songs and poems, and in his *Observations in the Art of English Poesie* (1602) controversially maintained that rhyme should be used sparingly: 'the facility and popularity of rhyme creates as many poets as hot summer flies'; he put emphasis on the pattern of accent.

p.46 'The Aftermath'

Line 21: 'euphrasy' – the white-bloomed plant Euphrasia or Eyebright, an old cure for all eye maladies

Line 32: the dove is a symbol of peace, and EB no doubt has in mind Gerard Manley Hopkins's poem of that name, which ends: 'And when Peace here does house / He comes with work to do, he does not come to coo, / He comes to brood and sit'; perhaps also the close of Hopkins's sonnet 'God's Grandeur', 'Because the Holy Ghost over the bent / World broods with warm breast and with ah! bright wings.'

p.47 'Rural Economy (1917)'

The poem's metaphors rest on the Greek legend of Jason the Argonaut, who to gain the Golden Fleece had to plough a field with fire-breathing oxen, and then sow it with dragon's teeth, which sprouted into soldiers. He defended himself by tricking them into fighting each other.

Line 3: Thule, or *ultima Thule* as it was called by ancient geographers, was the name for the northernmost country, beyond the borders of the known world.

Line 26: 'ruseful' became 'thoughtful' when the poem was reprinted as part of the supplement to *Undertones*.

p.49 'The Still Hour'

EB: Swain, M.C. was our Captain Quartermaster, but in the March Offensive of 1918 was Adjutant & killed. A character! unfrightenable.

Line 7: 'the lubber fiend' – this English folkloric figure appears in Milton's 'L'Allegro', line 110: 'Then lies him down the lubber fiend / And stretched out all the chimney's length, / Basks at the fire his hairy strength'. Bush glosses it as 'drudging spirit'. The same spirit goes by the name of 'Lob', the title and subject of a poem by Edward Thomas that Blunden would have known; Thomas calls him 'one of the lords of No Man's Land'. Edna Longley provides an illuminating entry on the poem in her annotated edition of Edward Thomas, *Collected Poems* (Tarset: Bloodaxe, 2008), pp. 211–23.

Line 47: RSM Arthur Daniels, killed in action 31 July 1917; EB describes him as 'kind, witty and fearless' in *Undertones*, Chapter XVII.

Line 60: Lieutenant Basil Swain, of whom EB writes in Chapter I of *Undertones*: 'Fear he respected, and he exemplified self-conquest'.

p.53 'A Dream'

Line 5: Pactolus was the river in which the gods allowed King Midas to wash off his golden curse, and afterwards the river always flowed over golden sands.

Line 6: in Claire Poynting's copy, EB crossed out 'gold sands amorous' and wrote 'golden sands turned lover' (*TDC*).

Line 16: perdu – lost, used in *King Lear* Act IV, Scene 7 by Cordelia, referring to Lear out on the heath as 'poor perdu!' *OED* gives the 18th-century meaning of 'a soldier placed in a position of special danger, or ordered on a forlorn hope'.

p.56 'Strange Perspective'

Line 1: perhaps EB had in mind the lines from Horace's Odes, III.29, 'Happy the man...'; Dryden's famous paraphrase runs:

> Happy the man, and happy he alone,
> He who can call today his own:
> He who, secure within, can say,
> Tomorrow do thy worst, for I have lived today.
> Be fair or foul or rain or shine
> The joys I have possessed, in spite of fate, are mine.
> Not Heaven itself upon the past has power,
> But what has been, has been, and I have had my hour.

Line 3: in later editions is followed by 'And turns very tansies, fire-flowers, tindery.'

p.57 'Two Voices'

EB: He: Capt. Wallace, our Adjutant. 'King Edward's Road'? Before the march to the Somme.

The poem was first published as 'The Survivors (1916)' in *Weekly Westminster*, 2 August 1924.

The 'kind of holiday feeling' inspired in the soldiers in August 1916 by the words 'going south' is referred to in *Undertones* Chapter VIII, and expanded upon in EB's 1929 essay, 'The Somme Still Flows':

> War is not all war, and there lies the heart of the matter. 'Going South' was at first more like a holiday adventure than the descent to the valley of the shadows. I still make myself pictures of that march, and could not guess at any summer days more enchanting. The very fact that, after ceaseless rumours and contradictions, we were now certainly destined for the Somme battle made us shut our minds to the future and embrace the present. (*Fall In, Ghosts*, p.63)

Lines 2–3: appeared as 'In the farm parlour cool and bare; / plain words, which in his hearers bred' in *Undertones* (1928), but were printed as the present version in *Poems 1914–1930*.

p.58 'Preparations for Victory'

EB: On the Ancre in the days preceding our attack on the Beaumont Ridge, 3 Sept. 1916.

The advance on Beaumont Ridge gained the British scarcely 20 yards, with heavy casualties.

Line 1: perhaps there is an echo here of Psalm 91, as it appears in the *Book of Common Prayer*: 'Thus to my soul of him I'll say, he is my fortress and my stay, / My God in whom I will confide. / His tender love and watchful care shall free thee from the fowler's snare, / And from the noisome pestilence...'

Line 17: Caliban – Prospero's slave in Shakespeare's *Tempest*

Line 23: 'Grey' is replaced by 'Pale' in *Undertones*.

p.59 'Zero'

EB: The first moments of the attack at Hamel.

The attack in September 1916 is described in Chapter IX of *Undertones*:

> The east was scarlet with dawn and the flickering gunflashes; I

thanked God I was not in the assault, and joined the subdued carriers nervously lighting cigarettes in one of the cellars, sitting there on the steps, studying my watch. The ruins of Hamel were crashing chaotically with German shells, and jags of iron and broken wood and brick whizzed past the cellar mouth. ... There were wounded Highlanders trailing down the road.

The title was altered to 'Come On, My Lucky Lads' in *Undertones*, which EB elsewhere noted as 'Worley's expression', referring to the Wiring Sergeant with whom EB kept in touch until Worley's death in 1954, and whom he regarded as one of the heroes of his memoir. In *Poems 1914–1930* the title reverts to 'Zero'. 'Zero time' is the time set for an attack.

Lines 2–4: 'sky' is later replaced by 'gloom' and 'dye' by 'bloom'.

Line 20: 'clothed and in his right mind' – Mark 5:15, about the man who had been possessed by devils and was restored to health by Jesus

See draft in the First World War Poetry Digital Archive at http://ww1lit. nsms.ox.ac.uk/ww1lit/items/show/9786 (accessed 3 March 2018).

p.60 'At Senlis Once'

EB: Senlis was a village of a few hundred people only. Our stay there was cut short. It was a damp gloomy day or two, when the thatch and plaster all seemed mouldy – and yet...

Line 1: from a chorus in Milton's *Samson Agonistes*, line 1268:

Oh how comely it is and how reviving
To the spirits of just men long oppressed,
When God into the hands of their deliverer
Puts invincible might...

p.61 'Pillbox'

EB: Again, the Menin Rd 'do'. We were in captured pillboxes etc.

Greening (pp.340–1) quotes from a letter to Worley written by EB in 1929: 'We are both miraculously preserved, if you think of the many occasions when there was nothing between us and the machinery of war'. He also reproduces the inscription in the copy of *Undertones* that EB gave to Worley: 'When this set of recollections was written I was in a far country... so, much was only half right and much was forgotten. If I could have had Frank Worley at that Japanese hotel in 1925 or 6, a real History of our early experience should have emerged.'

Line 3: It has been suggested that this conflates the Menin Road fighting in September 1917 (Chapter XXIII) with an incident from 1916, involving Sergeant F.A. Hoad from Eastbourne (Helen McPhail & Philip Guest, *On the Trail of the Poets of the Great War: Edmund Blunden*, Barnsley: Leo Cooper, 1999, p.69).

Line 9: 'a blighty' – 'a wound which [a Briton] hopes is serious enough to invalid him back to England [Blighty]. ...The word is said by some "authorities" to be derived from the Hindustani word, Belaiti, which means "something foreign" or "over-the-sea"' – according to Lorenzo N. Smith's *Lingo of No Man's Land, a World War I Slang Dictionary*, 1918 (reprinted in 2014 by the British Library, with an introduction by Julie Coleman).

Line 16: In Greek mythology, Charon ferries the souls of the dead across the Styx to Hades.

p.62 'The Welcome'

EB: In the smaller battle of the Menin Rd. at the end of Sept.1917.

An early draft of this poem can be seen in the First World War Poetry Digital Archive, at http://ww1lit.nsms.ox.ac.uk/ww1lit/collections/item/9285 (accessed 24 February 2018)

p.63 'The Ancre at Hamel'

Reprinted in *Undertones* as 'The Ancre at Hamel: Afterwards'.

Line 9: 'water' changed to 'river' in *Undertones*, then back again in *Poems 1914–1930*.

p.64 'Country Sale'

EB: This was a 'sketch from life'. I regret not buying an early Pilgrim's Progress which was among the oddments. Where? Somewhere near Lydgate.

Line 28: Thomas Baskett printed the *Book of Common Prayer* in various formats in the mid-18th century; Charles Lamb remarks in his *Essays of Elia* on the pictures in the edition of Baskett he was familiar with at Christ's Hospital.

p.66 'Winter: East Anglia'

EB: A Jack Daines poem [brother of Mary Daines]

The poem was first collected in *To Nature* under the title 'Winter Piece'. The earlier version ended:

> And, frost forgot, the chase grows hot
> > Till boys such spoil despise
> But the cornered weasel stands his ground,
> Shrieks at the dogs and boys set round,
> > And like a fighter dies.

p.67 'Midnight Skaters'

EB: Back to Congelow [the farmhouse rented by the Blunden family from 1904].

Greening (Plate 38) reproduces a sketch EB made to illustrate the poem, along with his note about his childhood experiences:

> …and about 1907 I was once or twice bold enough to go out with one or two of our labourers and their girls to a small pond in the hop-garden nearest us, on nights of great frost, & slide. (One or two of them skated, but I only in a Pickwickian sense.) The pond was commonly reputed terribly deep, whence 'gulfs of wonder', and the reflection of the hop-poles might be fancied to 'sound' or plumb those gulfs.

p.69 'Achronos'

The poem was first published in *Poetica*, March 1925 as 'Epochs'; then as 'Eras' when the poem was first collected in *Masks of Time*, and was altered to 'Achronos' – Greek, meaning 'timeless' – in *English Poems*, with minor revisions.

Line 14: perhaps EB was thinking here of the Middle English poem *Pearl*, whose author, like Blunden, was a father bereft of his daughter.

Line 15: the firstborn sons of the Egyptians, killed as recounted in Exodus.

p.69 'Warning to Troops'

EB: I was haunted by a music from the church door at Béthune.

Line 11: Psalm 58:4, 'they are like the deaf adder that stoppeth her ear'

p.70 'In a Country Churchyard'

EB's first daughter, Joy, was born in July 1919 and died in August aged 5 weeks, apparently from contaminated milk. 'This was a grief beyond anything I had felt in the War. It has never been quite overcome' (undated draft, quoted in *TDC*).

The poem has verbal echoes of *Hamlet* Act V, Scene 1 where Hamlet considers the skull of Yorick.

Line 43: 'strig' – stalk of any fruit or flower; 'twitch' – couch grass (Wright). In *Poems 1914–1930*, this line and l.44 are changed to: 'And bones like bits of hated quitch / Recount fate's plot.' 'Quitch' is also a name for couch grass, which grows stealthily and quickly.

Line 51: simoom – a hot, dust-laden wind blowing in the desert

p.72 'Solutions'

Line 13: Georges-Louis Leclerc, Comte de Buffon (1707–88), published 36 volumes of his *Histoire Naturelle*, which was widely translated into English.

p.73 'An Infantryman'

EB: Having nothing much to do one afternoon near Mailly (I think) James Cassels and I went for a long walk in the rain. The poem is on him. 1916.

EB writes in Chapter X of *Undertones* that he and Cassels 'were an affectionate pair and poetically minded'. They worked side by side in the battalion until Cassels transferred to the Royal Flying Corps in 1917. The Royal Sussex Regiment's archive has the annotated copy of *Undertones* EB inscribed to Cassels:

> his old friend wishes all that the Happy Warrior should have: no Raids, no Box Barrages, no sudden storms of Paper Warfare; but good Billets, a brisk Pony, various allowances, a sympathetic Quartermaster, and sunshine from Poperinghe to Péronne (Greening, p.314)

p.74 'Departure'

Line 5: Phoebus – god of the sun in Roman mythology

p.74 'The Match'

First published as 'The Prison' in *London Mercury*, May 1928, and in revised form in *Nation & Athenaeum*, 17 November 1928, before being collected in *Retreat*.

Line 7: 'oeillades' – amorous glances; again *King Lear* provides a reference, Act IV, Scene 5: 'She gave strange oeillades and most speaking looks to noble Edmund.'

p.75 'The Zonnebeke Road'

EB: Hard weather. Potijze trenches, and they were poor.

Line 14: 'chaps' – jaws or cheeks

Line 18: Haymarket was a communications trench near Potijze in the Ypres Salient, for walking cases only following a raid (*TDC*).

The last line of this version is an improvement on its original form in *Masks of Time*: 'And freeze you out with hate and save my brain.'

p.76 'Concert Party: Busseboom'

EB: This was as it actually happened, on an early spring evening in 1917, – the 47th Division I think gave the Revue, in a large hut not far from Vlamertinghe.

p.77 'Vlamertinghe: Passing the Château, July 1917'

EB: It was still a fine-looking Château, with a 12-inch battery close to the front view.

He describes it in *Undertones*, Chapter XX:

> [the road] took one presently through a gorgeous and careless mul-
> titude of poppies and sorrels and bull-daisies to the grounds of
> Vlamertinghe Château, many-windowed, not much hurt, but looking
> very dismal in the pitiless perfect sun. Its orchards yet clung to some
> pale apples, but the gunners were aware of that, the twelve-inch
> gunners, whose business seemed like a dizzy dream.

Line 1: Keats's 'Ode on a Grecian Urn', stanza 4:

> Who are those coming to the sacrifice?
> To what green altar, O mysterious priest,
> Leadst thou that heifer lowing at the skies,
> And all her silken flanks with garlands dressed?

Line 13: A draft of the poem shows that that EB had first written 'If you ask me, Vid…' then crossed out the name of his friend, substituting 'Jack'; replaced by 'mate' in the printed version. See http://ww1lit.nsms.ox.ac.uk/ww1lit/items/show/9722 (accessed 24 February 2018).

p.78 'Gouzeaucourt: the Deceitful Calm'

EB: We were taken out of the Passchendaele battle, at least out of the intolerable business of holding the ground taken, in Jan 1918, and went down to the 5th Army Front, which was to be overrun by the Germans on 21 March.

In early 1918, EB departed from Gouzeaucourt for six months' training in Suffolk. He writes in the last chapter of *Undertones*:

> One or two nights had been particularly anxious and bombarded
> ones, and the future here would evidently be much the same as that
> of Ypres. It was some comfort to be told that the battalion would be
> relieved in a night or two; in that belief, which was a delusion, I said
> good-bye and went away.

Line 18: 'greater' changed to 'plainer' in *Poems 1914–1930*, and in subsequent Penguin editions of *Undertones* to 'simpler'.

p.79 'La Quinque Rue'

EB: It was a strange road to a newcomer at night in '16.

Greening notes the changes made in subsequent editions of *Undertones* and in *Poems 1914–1930*, chiefly the addition of a line after line 20: 'What need of that stopped tread, that countersign?' and a change to the present line 22: 'I know your way of turning blood to glass'.

p.80 '"Trench Nomenclature"'

EB: These names were all real. I should like to collect more, for many were curious. Gunner's Siding. Crow's Nest. White City. Fifth Avenue. Over the Way. Oscar Copse and Wild Wood.

Line 3: Jacob's vision in Genesis 28:12: 'And he dreamed, and behold a ladder set up on the earth, and the top of it reached to heaven: and behold the angels of God ascending and descending on it.'

Line 4: 'Non Angli sed angeli...' (not Anglo-Saxons but angels) – words attributed to Pope Gregory when he saw British slave children in Rome in 573, here reversed.

Line 5: 'Brock's Benefits' were fireworks displays by the old-established manufacturers Brocks, put on regularly at the Crystal Palace in London from 1865 to 1936 (with a break 1910–20).

Line 7: 'Picturedrome' was an early cinema chain; Greening notes that one was built in West Sussex in 1914. J.M.W. Turner (1775–1851), the great painter of light effects on sea and land.

Line 14: 'Minnie' from *minenwerfer* – 'the German 198lb trench mortar high explosive shell... At night it has a tail of fire like a rocket. It kills by concussion' (*Lingo of No Man's Land*); 'quean' – badly behaved woman, or prostitute.

Line 17: 'What's in a name?' asks Juliet in *Romeo and Juliet*, Act II, scene 2.

p.81 'Another Journey from Béthune to Cuinchy'

EB: Imaginary dialogue between E.B. 1916 & E.B.1924 or later.

Cuinchy is a village midway between Béthune and La Bassée, where EB's battalion was active in May–June 1916.

Line 39: 'old Perpendicular' refers to the church spire in the Gothic style

Line 49: EB describes their HQ in Chapter IV of *Undertones*:

Kingsclere's shuttered windows, and masses of sandbags, looked better than C Company's cellar. Kingsclere had a cellar, too, a delicate retreat from the glaring heat-wave outside, and a piano in it, and marguerites and roses in jars on the table. But there was an air of anxiety and uncertainty about the headquarters staff as they came and went.

Line 55: darnel – rye grass

Line 60: 'don't mench!' – polite reply to the assumed thanks, 'Don't mention it!'

Line 64: 'red-hatted cranks' – Military Police were distinguished by an arm band and a red cap-cover hence their nickname Red Caps (*TDC*).

Line 67: *It's a Mad World, My Masters* was a proverbial phrase, and the title of a comedy by the Jacobean dramatist Thomas Middleton.

Line 73: British soldiers' daily rations in 1914 included '1/10 gill [142 ml]

lime juice if fresh vegetables not issued'; this was to keep scurvy at bay. (See https://wwi.lib.byu.edu/index.php/British_&_German_rations, accessed 22 February 2018)

Line 86: 'dagged' – clotted with dirt

Line 94: Coldstream Lane – EB describes the spot in Chapter IV of *Undertones*:

> Over Coldstream Lane, the chief communication trench, deep red poppies, blue and white cornflowers and darnel thronged the way to destruction; the yellow cabbage-flowers thickened here and there in sickening brilliance.

Line 111: 'shell' is changed to 'crump' in *Poems 1914–1930*.

p.85 'Flanders Now'

First published as 'Old Battlefields' in *Harper's Monthly Magazine*, March 1927.

p.87 'The Author's Last Words to His Students'

First published in *Japanese Garland* (London: The Beaumont Press, 1928).

After his initial dismay, EB found much to which he could respond in Japan. In his 1930 essay 'Japanese Moments' (*The Mind's Eye*, pp.89–96), he maintains that 'Japan does not disappoint the stranger; she corrects his fancies, perhaps a little grimly, and then begins to enrich him with her truths'; what he valued in his students was their responsiveness to the literature he taught, 'our imaginative inheritance is honoured'.

The Beaumont Press was run by Cyril W. Beaumont (1891–1976), a pioneer dance historian. At 19 he began to run the bookshop, bought for him by his father, at 75 Charing Cross Road. A severe knee injury prevented his being called up. In 1917 he decided to launch his own imprint: 'It seemed to me a pity that modern writers should not be afforded an opportunity of having their works published in a choice form during their lifetime.' He produced 26 books between 1917 and 1931. For example, Richard Aldington wrote to him from the trenches offering his poems, and these were published in 1919 as *Images of War*, alongside books by D.H. Lawrence and Herbert Read. He published Blunden's *To Nature* (1923), *Masks of Time* (1925), *Japanese Garland*, *A Summer's Fancy* (1930), and *To Themis* (1931), which was the final Beaumont Press publication; also Blunden's edition of newly discovered poems by John Clare, *Madrigals & Chronicles* (1924). These books were illustrated by Randolph Schwabe (1885–1948), a war artist in both wars and Slade Professor of Fine Art at University College London from 1930 until his death.

See Katherine Sorley Walker, 'Cyril W. Beaumont', *Dance Chronicle*, vol. 25, no. I; Gill Clarke, *Randolph Schwabe* (Bristol: Sansom & Co, 2012), which reproduces some of the illustrations for Blunden's collections.

p.89 'A Sunrise in March'

Line 10: Oliver Cromwell (1599–1658) was in charge of the cavalry in the New Model Army created in 1645 to fight against the army of King Charles I in the Civil War.

p.90 'The Kiln'

Line 4: In Shakespeare's *Timon of Athens*, the Athenian nobleman loses his fortune and after giving a final 'banquet' in his mansion, goes to live in a cave.

p.92 'The Deeper Friendship'

Line 4: 'my first-found joy' – the village of Yalding, his relationship with which he described as 'a love affair' (Webb, p.25)

p.94 'Report on Experience'

EB: 'Unpremeditated', & almost thrown away.

Line 1: cf. Psalm 37:25: 'I have been young, and now am old; yet have I not seen the righteous forsaken...' (This psalm also includes the words 'the meek shall inherit the earth', and 'For the arms of the wicked shall be broken: but the Lord upholdeth the righteous.') Also King Henry's words in Shakespeare's *Henry VI Part I*, Act III, Scene 5: 'When I was young, – as yet I am not old –'.

Line 9: Seraphina – possibly from *Martin Chuzzlewit*, where the same Psalm is quoted; see Greening's note in *Undertones* (p.279), where he also points out that on his return from Japan, EB discovered that his first wife had been having an affair.

p.95 'A Connoisseur'

Line 5: Merlin – the wizard who features in the Arthurian legend and medieval Welsh poetry.

Line 14: Squire Harkaway – perhaps taken from *London Assurance*, a comedy by Dion Boucicault, first produced in London in 1841.

Line 16: Croesus – last king of Lydia (modern-day Turkey) in the 6th century BC, who was renowned for his great wealth.

EB was a serious book-collector, but worked within a strict budget. His friend Rupert Hart-Davis wrote, 'He knew every edition of every book, important or obscure, the handwriting of every writer and of many lesser individuals, and he had a diviner's instinct of where treasure might lurk' (quoted by Webb, p.247).

p.97 'Into the Salient'

EB: We went north into the Ypres salient & town, and it was a little time before we knew how overlooked by the German positions every place was.

Line 1: sallows – small willow trees

Line 10: Hill 60 was manmade, literally 60 metres above sea level, and offered an important vantage point in the flat landscape south-east of Ypres. It was mined and shelled, and passed to and fro between the Germans and the Allies. (See http://www.firstworldwar.com/today/hill60.htm , accessed 22 February 2018.) EB was there in late February 1917, as he relates in Chapter XVII of *Undertones*.

p.98 'Premature Rejoicing'

EB: Illustrates my meeting with Realists in August 1916.

Line 5: Titania, the fairy queen in Shakespeare's *Midsummer Night's Dream*.

p.98 'To Joy'

This was first collected in *To Nature*, but in *Poems 1914–1930* Blunden replaced the original archaisms: 'My blood away to give thee warm / Thou ne'er on earth hast made one step, / …o' the storm.' He did in fact provide blood for a transfusion (*TDC*). There are poems in memory of the child scattered throughout EB's work; the composer Gerald Finzi set this one to music.

p.101 'Under a Thousand Words'

Line 4: La Boisselle was a notorious sector on the Western Front, where the French had stemmed the German advance in September 1914. While there was stalemate above ground, beneath it there was tunnelling by the French and Germans, and underground warfare. The area was known as the 'Glory Hole'. When the British took over the sector, they employed professional miners to deepen the tunnels; above, the infantry sides were separated by a mere 45 metres. At the start of the Battle of the Somme there were two massive mines, known as Y Sap and Lochnagar, flanking the village, but they did not neutralise the German defences and the 34th Division, attacking on 1 July, suffered the worst losses of any unit that terrible day. The ruins of La Boisselle were eventually captured by the British on 4 July. (See http://www.laboisselleproject.com/history accessed 21 February 2018.) EB refers to the village in his essay 'The Somme Still Flows'.

Lord Macaulay: Thomas Babington Macaulay's 'Epitaph on a Jacobite' begins 'To my true king I offered free from stain / Courage and faith; vain faith, and courage vain'; EB must also have been thinking of Macaulay's valiant 'Horatius', who 'kept the bridge / In the brave days of old.'

p.102 'The Sunlit Vale'

Published in the *London Mercury* (October 1929) as 'The Failure'.

Line 6: Sir Philip Sidney (1554–1586), flower of the Elizabethan age as poet, courtier, scholar and soldier, died of wounds received in the battle of Zutphen. As he lay dying, he is reported to have given water to another soldier, saying 'Thy necessity is greater than mine.'

p.103 'Incident in Hyde Park, 1803'

The poem is based on a true case, that of James Macnamara (1768–1826). He addressed the jury:

> Gentlemen, I am a Captain of the British Navy. My character you can only hear from others; but to maintain any character, in that station, I must be respected. When called upon to lead others into honourable danger, I must not be supposed to be a man who had sought safety by submitting to what custom has taught others to consider as a disgrace. […] I hope to obtain my liberty, through your verdict; and to employ it with honour in the defence of the liberties of my country.

https://www.oldbaileyonline.org/browse.jsp?id=t18030420-2&div=t1 8030420-&terms=macnamara (accessed 30 March 2018)

p.107 'The Kiss'

Line 20: 'kobold' – a spirit living in caves or mines in German folklore.

Last line: 'aconite' – a first flower of spring, the yellow winter aconite (Eranthis hyemalis).

p.110 'The Memorial, 1914–1918'

Greening's notes to this poem in his edition of *Undertones* are particularly illuminating. He points out that Sir Edward Lutyen's Thiepval Memorial to over 79,000 missing on the Somme opened a couple of months before the poem was published, but that Blunden may also have had in mind a more generic concept of WWI memorials. Sassoon derided the new Menin Gate as 'a pile of peace-complacent stone' after its unveiling in 1927 (quoted by Gavin Stamp in his fascinating study *The Memorial to the Missing of the Somme*, London: Profile Books, 2006, p.105).

Line 15: 'corons' – Greening suggests that this refers to the wreaths around the names of the battles or the dead.

Line 17: 'aether stream' – Greening notes that Broadcasting House had been opened in London in March of the same year, and that the idea of some emanation from beyond the grave was hugely influential during the War. The English physicist Sir Oliver Lodge, who helped develop radio, was convinced that the spirit world existed in the ether, and wrote about the consoling messages he received from his youngest son, who died at Ypres in 1915.

p.111 'November 1, 1931'

The date is EB's 35th birthday. The epigraph to *Halfway House* is Henry Cary's translation of the opening of Dante's *Inferno*: 'In the mid way of this our mortal life, / I found me in a gloomy wood astray…'

Line 14: Magdalen College, Oxford (EB was now teaching at Oxford); the Menin Gate – at the start of the route out of Ypres towards the front line, along the Menin Road. EB refers to the Gate in *Undertones* as 'that unlovely hiatus'.

p.112 'The Cottage at Chigasaki'

EB's note in *Choice or Chance*: Perhaps the most familiar Japanese poem is that which says, approximately, 'The morning-glory has taken hold of the well-bucket. I'll borrow some water elsewhere.'

The haiku to which he refers is by the Buddhist nun Chiyo-ni (1703–75). Chigasaki is on the coast, not far from Tokyo and Yokohama.

p.113 'Lark Descending'

Titled simply 'The Skylark' originally (see the draft reproduced in *TDC*), the poem was published in *Choice or Chance* under the title here. EB surely had in mind one of the most loved pieces of English music, *The Lark Ascending*, by Ralph Vaughan Williams; also the long poem of the same name by George Meredith, which inspired the composer and was much admired by Siegfried Sassoon. It is said that RVW composed the piece while watching troops embark in August 1914, but this has been disputed. It was first performed in public in 1920.

p.115 'At Rugmer'

Rugmer is in Yalding.

Line 6: 'kex' is noted in the *Dictionary of Sussex Dialect* as used in the extreme east of the county: the 'dry hollow stalk of hogweed, cow parsley and other umbelliferae'.

p.116 'An Ominous Victorian'

First published as 'An Eminent Victorian' in *The Spectator*, 17 November 1933. Lytton Strachey's *Eminent Victorians*, iconoclastic biographical studies of four of them, was published in 1918 and revolutionised the art of biography and the view of Victorians. In his revised title, EB suggests the fate in store for once revered literary figures.

Line 1: Eliza Cook (1818–89): her poetry was hugely popular with the working-class public in both England and America; her best-known poem was 'The Old Armchair'.

Line 6: Felicia Dorothea Hemans (1793–1835), poet; the opening lines of two of her poems are famous: 'The boy stood on the burning deck…' ('Casabianca') and 'The stately homes of England…' (parodied by Noel Coward).

Line 7: *It Is Never Too Late to Mend* (1856), a popular novel by Charles Reade

Line 32: Samuel Rogers, (1763–1855), a poet now best known for his friendship with more famous poets, and as a generous host to literary London. He first came to prominence with *The Pleasures of Memory* (1792).

p.119 'Writing a Sketch of a Forgotten Poet'

EB in his preface to *Poems 1930–1940*: 'The name of the forgotten poet […] was Mary Leapor, a most attractive young writer of the eighteenth century, and regarded as a prodigy because she was also the daughter of a gardener.' He wrote an article about her, 'A Northamptonshire poet: Mary Leapor', published in the *Journal of the Northamptonshire Natural History Society*, June 1936.

p.121 'Minority Report'

Line 8: Quintus Horatius Flaccus (65 BC–8 BC), known in the English-speaking world as Horace; a great Augustan lyric and satirical poet, he also served for a time in the Roman army.

p.123 'On a Picture by Dürer'

Sonnenuntergang – Weiher im Walde / Landscape with a Woodland Pool (c.1495): this watercolour by Albrecht Dürer is part of the collection of the British Museum, where perhaps EB saw it. The poem was first published in August 1936.

p.124 'Cricket, I Confess'

EB remarked in a letter from Japan to Philip Tomlinson in August 1949, 'If only these attentive and beauty-loving Japanese understood cricket!' (Webb, p.278) The cricketers he remembers were all in the 1909 England Ashes team: Albert Relf (1874–1937), who played for Sussex; Gilbert Jessop (1874–1955), who played for Gloucestershire; Kenneth Hutchings (1882–1916), who played for Kent and was reckoned to be the most talented English batsman of his era, killed on the Somme.

Line 5: 'Poor Tom, thy horn is dry' – Edgar in *King Lear*, Act III, Scene 6, has no more to say.

p.125 'To W.O. and His Kind'

EB was offered the chance of publication by Lord Carlow (1907–44), a keen book-collector and amateur typographer, whose private Corvinus Press published work by T.E. Lawrence, James Joyce and Walter de la Mare, among others. *On Several Occasions* was issued in an edition of 60 copies in April 1939, with 16 new poems including this one.

Last line: 'kindly' was later changed to 'genuine'.

p.127 'Company Commander, 1917'

VID: A.G. Vidler, an Old Blue (Christ's Hospital pupil), severely wounded in 1915 near Festubert; later commissioned in the Royal Sussex. Described by EB as 'an invincible soldier', he never fully recovered from his head wounds or the loss of his only brother near Arras in 1917, and committed suicide in 1924. EB's elegy 'A.G.A.V.' is included in *Undertones*.

Line 1: 'How lovely are the messengers...' an anthem by Felix Mendelssohn, taken from Isaiah 52:7

Line 11: 'O for the peace...' a Victorian hymn also known as 'A Little While', by Jane Crewdson

p.129 'What is Winter?'

First published as 'A Day in December', *Poetry Review* [Jan/Feb] 1943.

p.132 'Thoughts of Thomas Hardy'

Line 11: threne – threnody

EB wrote an account of his literary life, *Thomas Hardy* (1942). He had met Hardy several times at the poet's home, Max Gate, introduced by Siegfried Sassoon in 1922. Sassoon felt that the two poets were uncannily similar: 'They share a sort of old-fashioned seriousness about everything connected with authorship. Both are fundamentally countrified and homely. Even in outward appearance they have a similarly bird-like quality. ... Also both are essentially modest and unassuming' (Webb, pp.133–4). After a visit in 1923 EB recorded that Hardy's 'talk is a mixture of trifles with which old age amuses itself, and details of real importance in reading his life – e.g. his first serious reading book (Dryden's *Virgil*), and his zest for discussing smugglers and soldiers' (Webb, p. 135). EB's vivid 'Notes on Visits to Thomas Hardy' were reprinted in *Edmund Blunden: A Selection of His Poetry and Prose*, edited by Kenneth Hopkins (London: Rupert Hart-Davis, 1950). Mrs Hardy presented EB with Hardy's own copy of Edward Thomas's *Poems* as a memento in 1926.

p.133 'The Vanishing Land'

Line 7: abeles – white poplars

p.135 'After the Bombing'

In 1947 EB was invited by the Foreign Office to go to Japan as part of a liaison mission, and he stayed there until 1950, with his wife and young family. He had written to his brother in August 1945 that the bombing 'will have strengthened the feeling of all the Orient from Persia onward that the Western Civilisation is *the* barbarism. [...] So any of us who can help at all in reviving the message of men like Shelley and Henry Vaughan should not miss any opening' (Webb, p.272).

p.138 'High Elms, Bracknell'

The poem refers to the house in which Shelley and his wife Harriet lived for a few months in 1813, with their baby, Ianthe. The marriage of the 19-year-old poet and his 16-year-old bride did not last. EB visited the house near Windsor with Claire when he was writing his biography of Shelley, published in 1946. The two buds were 'poppies which Claire pressed into her copy of *Shelley*' and have remained there (*TDC*).

p.142 'C.E.B.'

This elegy for his father was written two years after the death of Charles Edmund Blunden, whom EB describes in 'An Empty Chair' as 'A Sussex man but domiciled in Kent / And loving those earth-skills (thought so little of)/ By which the whole's sustained'; schoolmaster, musician and cricketer.

p.143 'At the Great Wall of China'

EB travelled to China with a group from the University of Hong Kong in December 1955. As well as the comparison with sentries in WWI, the title recalls '"Trench Nomenclature"', and a resonant incident in *Undertones* Chapter XVIII, where in the 'Great Wall of China' trench Blunden met a sentry who 'spoke, grinned and shivered; we passed; and duly the sentry was hit by a shell.'

p.144 'A Hong Kong House'

The poem was first published in 1955 when EB was teaching at the University of Hong Kong. His daughter describes the house, which has since been pulled down: 'The garden was overlooked by a long veranda which ran the length of the side of EB's house. It was an informal garden, dominated by a soaring palm tree, which looked down to the university buildings and the sea beyond. [...] playthings – refers to his daughters' toys left on the lawn.' (*TDC*)

p.145 'Millstream Memories'

Line 3: Macbeth to the ghost of Duncan, 'Avaunt, and quit my sight', *Macbeth*, Act III, scene 4

Lines 4–5: an echo of Edgar disguised as a madman, 'Fraterretto calls me and tells me Nero is an angler in the lake of darkness' (*King Lear*, Act III, Scene 6) – fishing in Hell must have been a peculiarly resonant image for EB.

p.146 'Dog on Wheels'

Explaining that her youngest sister had this toy to push around when she was learning to walk, Margi Blunden sees the poem as emblematic of her father's isolation amidst a young family and the busy life of Hong Kong in the later 1950s: 'His "battered" face carries its difficult history from the war. [...] The sadness invested in the dog in the final two lines reflects something of his own feelings about his situation at this time.' (Margi Blunden, *My Father, Edmund Blunden*, London: Cecil Woolf, 2011, p.8)

p.148 'Darkness'

Written when the Blitz was continuing in London, and severe in Plymouth, Swansea, Glasgow and Liverpool. Britain was very isolated, with the USSR not an ally until June and the USA disengaged until the end of 1941. Lines 6–7: EB draws on Prospero's farewell speech, 'Our revels now are ended', *The Tempest*, Act 4, Scene 1.

p.149 'A Swan, A Man'

Written in 1964. The setting is the old mill pool next to Hall Mill (in Long Melford, Suffolk), the house where EB retired (*TDC*).

Line 16: The Ancient Mariner of Coleridge's poem is cursed with unquenchable memory, and advises his listeners, 'He prayeth best, who lovest best / All things both great and small'.

p.150 'Ancre Sunshine'

Published in *Garland* (Cambridge: the Golden Head Press, 1969).

This was the last poem EB wrote, probably during a visit to the battlefields, and *TDC* notes that 'it has the distinction of being the last poem about the war written by any surviving soldier poet.'

He closed an essay on 'Yalding Bridges' from 1931: 'I suppose I liked the River Ancre between Hamel and Thiepval in the autumn of a year of holocausts because it resembled this little nook of our village. In my dreams nowadays they merge into an identity, and shells just miss the alders of Cheveney-lez-Miraumont' (*The Mind's Eye*, p.175).

Line 11: His wife Claire represents for him a later generation.

Line 12: Miraumont was a village north of Grandcourt, taken from the Germans by the British in February 1917, and completely destroyed in the course of the war.

NOTES TO 'GOING OVER THE GROUND AGAIN'

1. *Selected Letters*, 1, p.124 (24 August 1926).
2. See http://www.westminster-abbey.org/our-history/people/poets-of-the-first-world-war (accessed 13 April 2018)
3. Jay Winter, *Remembering War: the Great War between memory and history in the twentieth century* (New Haven & London: Yale University Press, 2006), p.1.
4. Paul Fussell, *The Great War and Modern Memory* (Oxford University Press, 1975), p.254.
5. 'Edmund Blunden writes...' *Poetry Book Society Bulletin*, no. 14 (May 1957).
6. The literary 'loyalties' were exactly that, scholarly and long-lasting. Brownlee Kirkpatrick's *Bibliography of Edmund Blunden* (Oxford: Clarendon Press, 1979) records over 50 entries for books, articles and reviews on Lamb, 45 for his beloved Clare, 40 for Coleridge; Shelley, something of an obsession, accounts for over 60; and Keats, another, for over 50. No doubt there are echoes and quotations that have not been identified in the notes to this selection; they will have come from EB's extensive and repeated reading of these authors' prose as well as poems.
7. Siegfried Sassoon, *Siegfried's Journey* (London: Faber & Faber, 1945), p.146.

8. Eric J. Leed, *No Man's Land: combat and identity in World War I* (Cambridge University Press, 1979), p. 122.

9. *Poems by Ivor Gurney: principally selected from unpublished manuscripts*, with a memoir by Edmund Blunden (London: Hutchinson, 1954), p.11.

10. *The Great War and Modern Memory*, p.269. Fussell ends the chapter with a nice example of the 'calendar-art sentiments' Blunden's approach risked and avoided.

11. Renato Poggioli, *The Oaten Flute: essays on pastoral poetry and the pastoral ideal* (Cambridge, Mass: Harvard University Press, 1975), p.7, makes this point. EB refers to Walton in his essay on his love of bookbindings, 'Bringing them Home':

> My taste probably began in childhood… Isaak Walton was festooned with golden creels and rods and lines and trout and bulrushes; the old man himself, on what I think they call the back strip (so one might speak of an angel's vertebrae), stood forever there by the hawthorn bush, baiting his hook, about to throw in again. (*The Mind's Eye*, pp.232–3)

12. Peter V. Marinelli, *Pastoral* (London: Methuen, 1971), p.2. EB compiled a collection of Wordsworth's poems for young readers, *The Solitary Song*, published by the Bodley Head in 1970. See also Robert Hemmings, 'Landscape as palimpsest: Wordsworthian topography in the war writings of Blunden and Sassoon', *Papers on Language & Literature*, vol. 43, no. 3 (2007), which explores the significance of maps and map-reading for Blunden.

13. In a review essay, 'The Preservation of Rural England', Blunden refers to the English as 'tenants of this genuine Arcadia', under threat from post-war developers. Published in the *TLS* March 1929; reprinted in Edmund Blunden, *Votive Tablets* (London: Cobden-Sanderson, 1931), p.352.

14. *Selected Letters*, 1, p.7 (18 September 1920).

15. Robert H. Ross, *The Georgian Revolt; the rise and fall of a poetic ideal 1910–1922* (London: Faber & Faber, 1967), p.187.

16. Edna Longley, 'War Pastorals' in Tim Kendall ed., *The Oxford Handbook of British and Irish War Poetry* (Oxford University Press, 2007), p.466.

17. Longley, 'War Pastorals', p.467.

18. Edna Longley, 'The Great War, history, and the English lyric' in Vincent Sherry, ed. *The Cambridge Companion to the Literature of the First World War* (Cambridge University Press, 2005), p.79.

19. Marinelli, *Pastoral*, p.9.

20. Longley, 'The Great War, history, and the English lyric', pp.78–9.

21. Webb, p.84.

22. Blunden wrote to Sassoon on 22 July 1926, 'I can still smell shelling and chloride of lime – but I can't remember the base; nor the long journeys to and fro from leave. Sometimes a sausage balloon hanging over Tokyo gives me an awkward feeling' (*Selected Letters*, 1, p.121).

23. Quoted by Webb, pp.118–19.

24. Blunden's modesty was remarked on by everyone who knew him. The poet Vernon Scannell, in his memoir *A Proper Gentleman*, described him as 'the most modest, courteous and generous man I have ever met or will be likely to meet and it was impossible not to love him' (quoted by Webb, p.317).

25. Blunden to Sassoon, 24 August 1926: 'Yet, I think there are two things to be considered in this "game of ghosts": not only how the man felt then towards his "present," but how he feels now towards his "present." He may choose the time when he *was* necessary, (roughly) effective, and felt friendship about him' (*Selected Letters*, 1, p.123).

26. Hardy noted that Egdon Heath, the setting of *Return of the Native*, 'may be the heath of that traditionary King of Wessex – Lear'; Shakespeare's Lear is a recurring presence in Blunden's war writing. See the discussion of this in Desmond Graham, *The Truth of War: Owen, Blunden and Rosenberg* (Manchester: Carcanet Press, 1984), pp.93–6. For EB's relationship with Hardy, see p.169 n.9; p.191 note to p.132.

27. He subsequently altered the verb in line 3 to 'Foreheads still trenched with feverish wonderings', perhaps thought it was too obvious a metaphor and in *Poems 1914–1930* – where it closes the section 'War: impacts and delayed actions' – changed the line to 'Foreheads entrenched with all the argument'.

28. A phrase used by Peter Scupham in his generally very appreciative essay, 'Edmund Blunden', *PN Review*, vol, 25 no.3 (January–February 1999), p.61.

29. Fussell, *The Great War and Modern Memory*, p.268.

30. Edmund Blunden*, War Poets 1914–1918*, published for the British Council and the National Book League (Harlow: Longmans, Green & Co., 1958; reprinted with additions to the bibliography 1964, 1969), p.11.

31. Longley, 'The Great War, history, and the English lyric', p.65.

32. Rothkopf notes that for Blunden and Sassoon, 'T.S. Eliot became a focus of their distaste for Modernist poetry. A kind of sniper fire fills these letters, directed chiefly at Eliot and his acolytes.' She suggests that 'Blunden was perhaps more distressed than he said outright by Eliot's dismissal of his preference for the countryside, Lamb and Vaughan as signs of immaturity' in a *Dial* review of September 1927 (*Selected Letters*, 1, pp. xxiv, xxix n.27).

33. Jon Silkin, *Out of Battle: the poetry of the Great War* (Oxford University Press, 1972), p.110.

34. Sarah Cole, *Modernism, Male Friendship, and the First World War* (Cambridge University Press, 2003), p.14. In an interview with John Press, EB remarked mildly, 'I daresay I could find free verses of mine before I was conscious of many modern free-verse writers. The First World War did something to shake us up on forms and metres, and generally on the music of verse.' Peter Orr, ed., *The Poet Speaks; interviews with contemporary poets* (London, Routledge & Kegan Paul, 1966, pp.33–7), p.34.

35. Quoted by Webb, p.144.

36. Greening, introduction to *Undertones*, p.lxvii. The poem in this selection

perhaps least easily identifiable as Blunden's is 'Into the Salient' (p.97), and it is one of the few he wrote in free verse.

37. Michael Roberts, ed., *The Faber Book of Modern Verse* (London: Faber, 1936), p.1. Also omitted for this reason were Charles Sorley, Walter de la Mare, Edwin Muir, William Plomer and Roy Campbell, whom Roberts lists; he does not mention (or include) Robert Frost or Edward Thomas.

38. F.R. Leavis, *New Bearings in English Poetry* (1932; Harmondsworth: Pelican Books, 1972), pp.53–4.

39. Quoted by Webb, pp.43–4, from the introduction to Philip Longworth, *The Unending Vigil: a history of the Commonwealth War Graves Commission* (London: Constable, 1967).

40. War had been 'overwhelmingly found out' on the Somme for this *ancien combatant*, as he wrote in 1929: 'What men did in the battle of the Somme, day after day, and month after month, will never be excelled in honour, unselfishness, and love; except by those who come after and resolve that their experience shall never again fall to the lot of human beings.' (*Fall In, Ghosts*, p.66) EB wrote to Sassoon on 13 April 1935: 'Do not be alarmed by Hitler! I feel sure he is a good hand once you get at him, and will be at the old X-roads at the exact time with the rations, as he undertook. I refuse to believe in Wars […]'. The facetious tone changed, but EB was still seeing the Second World War through the lens of the First: 'The *Strand Magazine* has asked me to "send some war poems" – "if possible early next week." B—r them all, say I. […] ("We have no quarrel with the German People" – was there ever a phrase which will mean so little in three months time? German soldiers are merely doing what they are told. But they'll all be "Huns" by Xmas.) Obviously it wouldn't do for them to *win*. I share the universal abhorrence of Hitler's methods and intentions.' (*Selected Letters*, 2, p.113; p.238, 18 September 1939)

41. Letter to Douglas quoted in Desmond Graham, *Keith Douglas 1920–1944 – a biography* (Oxford University Press, 1974), p.218n. In 'War Pastorals', Edna Longley suggests that 'Blunden's intermittent power to stand back and strip away deceit may have influenced Keith Douglas's desert pastoral' (p.472). Curiously, stationed in Egypt in 1942, Douglas discovered that his commanding officer had been Blunden's in 'the last show', and reported that Clarke had said: 'Marvellous feller, always bringin' me reports in astonishin'ly neat handwritin', astonishin'ly neat. And then he'd dish in a bit of astonishin'ly good poetry, too. Well, you'd better write and tell him I'm still tickin' over, what? Good.' *The Letters*, edited by Desmond Graham (Manchester: Carcanet Press, 2000), p.217.

42. Blunden, 'Siegfried Sassoon's Poetry', *The Mind's Eye*, pp. 272, 267. EB here adapts Lewis Carroll: 'I said it very loud and clear: / I went and shouted in his ear' ('Humpty Dumpty's Recitation'). I am indebted to the stimulating discussion of the truth of war poetry (and much else) in Edna Longley, 'The compact essential real truth', *Under the Same Moon: Edward Thomas and the English lyric* (London: Enitharmon, 2017), pp.121–76.

43. Keith Douglas, 'Poets in This War' in *The Letters*, pp.352–3.

44. Philip Larkin, 'The War Poet', reprinted from the *Listener* in *Required*

Writing: miscellaneous pieces 1955–1982 (London: Faber & Faber, 1983, pp.159–63), p.159.

45. Blunden in *Selected Letters*, 3, p.248 (25 October 1963).

46. These terms are taken from James Campbell's important essay 'Combat Gnosticism: the Ideology of First World War Poetry Criticism' (*New Literary History*, vol.30, Winter 1999, pp.203–15), which questions the privileging of combat experience in writing about war, especially as it affects literary criticism and anthologising.

47. Jay Winter, *Remembering War*, pp.52–3, 57.

48. This persistence of themes has been recognised in Martin Taylor's ordering and range of Blunden's poems in *Overtones of War: poems of the First World War* (London: Duckworth, 1996), and in John Greening's additional poetic supplement to his edition of *Undertones of War*.

49. Quoted by Paul Edwards, 'British war memoirs' in Vincent Sherry, ed. *The Cambridge Companion to the Literature of the First World War* (Cambridge University Press, 2005, pp. 15–33), p.28.

50. Blunden writes to Sassoon on 2 January 1931 that he experiences 'asthmatic accessions, which, when I sleep, are transformed into the most dreadful dreams of War – that is, I am in those dreams an utter coward and the battalion including me is about to raid' (*Selected Letters*, 1, p.311). Blunden was awarded the Military Cross for 'conspicuous gallantry in action' on the Somme in 1916, having just turned 20.

The role of dreams and the recognition of their peculiar character within PTSD is discussed by Cathy Caruth in various publications on trauma. She has pointed out that Freud had shell-shocked patients whose dreams returned and could not be 'understood in terms of any wish or unconscious meaning, but is, purely and inexplicably, the literal return of the event against the will of the one it inhabits' (introduction to *Trauma: explorations in memory*, Baltimore: Johns Hopkins University Press, 1995, p.5). The idea that the traumatic event has 'literally no place' in the past or the present makes it into a kind of no-man's-land in itself.

51. Margi Blunden, *My Father, Edmund Blunden: on Rereading* Undertones of War (London: Cecil Woolf, 2011), p.8.

52. Jay Winter, *War and Remembrance*, p.70.

53. In 1929, Blunden wrote, 'where the traditions and government which [the war] had called into being had ceased to be, we who had been brought up to it were lost men. Strangers surrounded me. No tried values existed now'('Aftertones', *Fall In, Ghosts*, p.59). These were young men when the war ended, and Blunden returned to that point in 1958: '… one trouble that followed was that peace was not all happiness; then millions of veterans (in their 'twenties) began looking back to such moments as that in the barn [in a poem by Sassoon] with desire and longing. At least there had been a generosity, a unity, a trust' (*War Poets 1914–1918*, p.28).

54. Tim Kendall, Introduction to *The Oxford Handbook of British and Irish War Poetry*, p.2.

Cathy Caruth asks: 'in what way is the experience of trauma also the experience of an imperative to live? What is the nature of a life that continues beyond trauma?' (*Literature in the Ashes of History*, Baltimore: Johns Hopkins University Press, 2013, p.7).

55. These concepts from Margalit's *The Ethics of Memory* (Cambridge, Mass: Harvard University Press, 2002) are explained in Jay Winter, *Remembering War*, pp.240–42.

56. Eric J. Leed, *No Man's Land: combat and identity in World War I*, pp. 79; p.113 quoting from C.E. Carrington, *Soldiers from the Wars Returning* (London, 1965), p.252.

57. It is interesting that although Blunden wrote in the 'Preliminary' to *Undertones* that the book was 'almost useless' because either most of its readers would have gone through the same experience and know it all, or a few readers would not have and '*neither will they understand*', when the second edition came out in 1930, he was able to say 'it has been read and understood by many'. See Greening's edition for the later prefaces.

58. *Poems by Ivor Gurney*, p.11.

59. Quoted by David Reynolds, *The Long Shadow: the Great War and the Twentieth Century* (London: Simon & Schuster, 2013), p.344. Reynolds agrees that Blunden 'left an indelible mark on our understanding of what constitutes "war poetry"'.

Index of First Lines